THE HEART OF MARY

THE HEART OF GOD

Reflections on the Necessary Role
of the
Immaculate Heart of Mary
In Today's World

By
Deacon Frank J. Shaughnessy

Nihil Obstat: Rev. Peter Drilling, Th.D.
            Censor Librorum

Imprimatur: Most Rev. Edward U. Kmiec, D.D.
            Bishop of Buffalo
            January 28, 2008

The "nihil obstat" and the "imprimatur" are official declarations that a book or pamphlet is free of doctrinal or moral error. No implication is contained therein that those who have granted the "nihil obstat" and "imprimatur" agree with the contents, opinions or statements expressed.

THE HEART OF MARY TO THE HEART OF GOD
By Deacon Frank J. Shaughnessy

isbn: 1-59330-555-9

Printed in the United States of America

THE HEART OF MARY
TO
THE HEART OF GOD

❧

By
Deacon Frank J. Shaughnessy

Aventine Press

ACKNOWLEDGEMENTS

This little work is dedicated to The Immaculate Heart of Mary with the hope that she will see fit with her powerful prayers to make the contents well known and well lived.

Thank you:

To my wife, Barbara, especially, for her loving patience and endurance during the considerable length of time that was needed to complete this.

To **all of our eight children and their spouses** for their continued support and encouragement. **Special thanks to Mary Rose and Jean Marie** for their wonderful work in preparing the manuscript for publication and carrying out everything that was needed for the final printing.

To Father Albert Roux, the National Director of the Marian Movement of Priests, for his assistance in editing and for his overall helpful suggestions and guidance.

To Monsignor Richard Nugent, the former pastor of St. Bernadette's Parish in Orchard Park, New York, whose spiritual direction and guidance helped greatly to bring about the final result.

To the members of the two Cenacles of the Marian Movement of Priests, of which my role has been as Spiritual Director, for their support and encouragement.

To the members of the Charismatic Prayer Group in Sts. Peter and Paul Parish in Hamburg, New York, of which I am Spiritual Director, for the continued support of their prayers.

To all for the help of your prayers.

TABLE OF CONTENTS

⌘

INTRODUCTION

The implementation of the message of Fatima is of vital importance to the world today. Pope John Paul II indicated this very strongly when he said, " Mary's message of Fatima is still more relevant than it was 65 years ago. It is still more urgent".[1] This message is about the salvation of souls, devotion to the Immaculate Heart of Mary, conversion of life, praying the Rosary and reparation to the Immaculate Heart of Mary. This collection of Reflections attempts to develop this message in relation to the reported interior locutions given by the Blessed Virgin Mary to Father Stefano Gobbi of the Marian Movement of Priests from 1973 to 1997, [2,3,4,5,6], the Marian spiritual doctrine of St. Louis de Montfort and the method of spiritual childhood of St. Therese of the Child Jesus. [7]

Also attempted is to help prepare people for an intermediate coming of Jesus. As will be explained, this is not the final coming of Jesus which will be immediately followed by the Last Judgment, but an intermediate coming which will be followed by a period of peace. This coming is in complete conformity with the teaching of the Catholic Church.

Also included as a follow-up to these Reflections is a Method of Consecration to the Sacred Heart of Jesus through Entrustment to the Immaculate Heart of Mary, including several pages as to how this may be accomplished through enrollment in the Community of the Servants of the Immaculate Heart of Mary.

St. Louis de Monfort's Act of Consecration to Jesus through Mary is presented here since this Act is highly recommended for those who wish to become members of the Community of the Servants of the Immaculate Heart of Mary.

Also included as a help to the praying of the Rosary with Mary's Heart are meditations on the Joyful, Luminous, Sorrowful and Glorious mysteries. Since there is a great emphasis in the Reflections on human life realities such as abortion, also included are Immaculate Heart pro-life meditations on the four sets of Rosary mysteries.

There are repetitions in these reflections of certain matters, such as e.g., some of the happenings at Fatima, the Cana event and St. Paul's statements about the victory of Jesus Christ in 1Corinthians, among others. They were repeated because they were considered necessary to that particular reflection.

Let us ask the Holy Spirit to guide and protect this work so that it may be a means of inspiring people to Consecrate themselves to the Sacred Heart of Jesus through Entrustment to the Immaculate Heart of Mary.

Come Holy Spirit, through the powerful intercession
of the Immaculate Heart of Mary, Your well beloved spouse!

<u>Author's Note</u> Re: The Marian Movement of Priests and the reported messages to Don Stefano Gobbi from the Blessed Virgin Mary contained in the book, *To The Priests, Our Lady's Beloved Sons, The Marian Movement of Priests, St. Francis Maine, 2000,* the following quote is presented:

Pope Urban VIII--- "In cases which concern private revelation, it is better to believe than not to believe, for if it is believed and it is proven true, you will be happy that you have believed, because our Holy Mother asked it, and if it should be proven false, you will receive all blessings as if it had been true, because you believed it to be true." (Internet-- Google--Cardinal Ratzinger and the Marian *Movement of Priests,* #9)

Also, it can be stated that there are at least 400 Bishops and a number of Cardinals who, worldwide, are members of the Marian Movement of Priests, more than 100,000 priests and millions of lay people and religious. In the United States as of 2000, there were 63,000 members, including 4000 clergy, Bishops, Priests and Deacons, Diocesan Priests from all 50 states, Religious and Lay People. (Internet--Google--*The Marian Movement of Priests,* #2, History of MMP)

The book, *To The Priests, Our Lady's Beloved Sons,* has the Imprimatur of Donald W. Montrose, D.D., Bishop of Stockton, Feb. 2, 1998, and that of Cardinal Bernardino Echeverria, O.F.M., Archbishop Emeritus of Guayaquil and Apostolic Administrator of Ibarra, who recommended the reading of these messages which he said "will contribute to the spread of devotion to our Lady".

NOTES

1. Pope John Paul II, at Fatima, May 13, 1982.
2. Lest there be any misunderstanding about the nature of interior locutions, "---the messages contained in this book, *To The Priests, Our Lady's Beloved Sons,* (TTPOLBS) which contains all of the reported messages to Father Gobbi, from 1973 to 1997, must not be understood as words spoken directly by Our Lady, but received in the form of interior locutions". (in front of book, on back of page containing photo of Pope John Paul II and statue of Our Lady of Fatima.)
3. "In the case of an authentic phenomenon , the interior locution is defined as that gift by which God wishes to make something known and to help someone carry something out as well as the outward clothing of this gift, in terms of human thoughts and words, according to the style and the way of writing of the person who receives the message." (TTPOLBS, p. xxxvII)
4. "--it (an interior locution) is not something strange or sensational, but a mystical phenomenon present in the life of the Church and described in manuals of spiritual theology. It is not sensorial communication with Jesus, our Lady or the saints such as takes place in authentic apparitions." (TTPOLBS, p.xxxvI)
5. "--St. John of the Cross calls locutions, or formal supernatural words, those distinct words which the spirit receives not from itself but from another person, sometimes while it is recollected and sometimes when it is not." (TTPOLBS) pp. xxxvII
6. "In reading this diary, which for many priests has already become a book for daily reflection, each sentence must be accepted with discernment,---. Let us consider, for example, Our Lady's advice to give up newspapers and television. For some, this may be interpreted literally. For many priests, it means, rather, not wasting precious hours, following programs that are frivolous and tendentious, etc.---." (TTPOLBS) p.xlII
7. TTPOLBS, p. xxxv

All Scripture texts are taken from *THE NEW AMERICAN BIBLE,* St. Joseph Edition, Catholic Book Publishing Co., New York, 1991

CHAPTER
I

THE PRESENCE
OF MARY TODAY

Mary's presence on earth today is being emphasized more than at any time in the history of the Church. Pope John Paul II's Encyclical, **Mother of the Redeemer**, which was written to mark the beginning of the Marian Year, emphasizes the "active and exemplary presence in the life of the Church" of Mary.[1] He refers to the presence of Mary today numerous times and indicates the different expressions this presence has; "through the faith and piety of individual believers, through the traditions of Christian families or 'domestic churches', of parish and missionary communities, religious institutes and dioceses, through the radiance and attraction of the great shrines".[2] The Holy Father also indicates that the Church sees Mary as "maternally present and sharing in the many complicated problems which today beset the lives of individuals, families and nations".[3]

The Presence of Mary on Earth Through Her Appearances

According to some Marian scholars there was a definite increase in the appearances of Mary on earth through apparitions, locutions and the like during the 20th century. During this century there were 386 claimed Marian apparitions. Of this number, 8 have been approved by the Catholic Church in such places as Portugal (Fatima), Belgium (2), Japan (Akita), Italy, Egypt, the Philippine Islands (Manila) and Venezuela. An additional 11 have been approved by the local Bishop for prayer and devotion at the site and 79 have been disapproved. This leaves 188 for which no final Church evaluation has been issued.[4]

Belief in the messages of these latter apparitions may still be valid for Catholics and may be helping them to grow spiritually but the individual Catholic must be willing to submit to a final evaluation by the Church if that should be given.

The importance of the time in which we live was set out in a prophetic manner by Karol Cardinal Wojtyla, the future Pope John Paul II, on November 9, 1976, in a visit to the United States. He said, "We are now standing in the face of the greatest historical confrontation humanity has gone through. I do not think that the wide circle of American society or wide circles of the Christian community understand this fully. We are now facing the final confrontation between the Church and anti-church, of the Gospel versus the anti-gospel".[5]

Why are the appearances of Mary increasing throughout the world? According to this statement by the future Pope, it would have to be concluded that the appearances of Mary have to be related to this final confrontation of which he speaks. It seems that people, as never before in history, are experiencing a great spiritual hunger and the need to fulfill that hunger. Also, God has a message for the people of the world which He wants them to hear. This message appears to be basically what was revealed at Fatima, Portugal in 1917 and at Akita, Japan in 1969-73. **This seems to be that hell is a reality, that many souls are being lost in hell through serious sins, and that this causes Jesus and Mary great sorrow.** At Fatima, in the apparition of July 13, 1917, this sorrow is shown in the face of Mary, according to Lucia, the oldest visionary. Mary showed the children a vision of hell. The children were terrified and in the words of Lucia, **"--Our Lady, who said to us so kindly and sadly: 'You have seen hell where the souls of poor sinners go. To save them God wishes to establish in the world devotion to my Immaculate Heart".**[6]

In the messages, Mary has revealed what people must do for their own personal salvation and that of others and what must be done to stop this flow of souls going to hell. This includes conversion of life, the necessity of prayer, the importance of the Sacraments of the Eucharist and Reconciliation, the importance of the Rosary, the value of penance, fasting and personal sacrifices in general, the necessity of reparation to God and to the Immaculate Heart of Mary and Consecration to the Heart of Jesus Christ through the Immaculate Heart of Mary.

Vatican II and the Presence of Mary on Earth

At the beginning of Vatican II, there arose a controversy concerning the place of Mary in the Council documents. There was no question that the Church Fathers wanted something to be set forth on Mary. The question was, should there be a separate document which would stress her relationship with Jesus or should the material on Mary be included in the document on the Church which would focus on her relationship with the Church? In a close vote it was decided that whatever was written about her would be placed in the document on the Church. Chapter 8 of the document, ***On the Church (LumenGentium),*** *The Role Of The Blessed Virgin Mary, Mother of God, In The Mystery Of Christ And The Church*, was then devoted to Mary.

At the end of Vatican II, Pope Paul VI accentuated Mary's relationship with the Church by declaring her to be **"Mother of the Church"**.[7] The Holy Spirit is the guiding force behind Vatican II and the Spirit is saying to the Church through this Council that our relationship with Mary today should be more focused on her presence as a member of the Church on earth, as one of us, as herself being a disciple of Jesus, indeed as our leader and role model in following Jesus. As one of us, she is beside us, helping us, sharing in all aspects of our daily lives, our joys our sorrows, our successes, our failures, in everything we do and in all that happens to us. We are being urged to see her as with us at all times.

Traditionally, our view of Mary has been one of seeing her in heaven as Queen of all the saints and angels and continually interceding with her Son, Jesus. The Fathers of the Church, in line with this, exhort us in Chapter 8 of ***On the Church*** to indeed pour forth persevering prayer to Mary in heaven as our Mother and the Mother of God,[8] which we should do. But the

Holy Spirit through the Council document and Pope John Paul II through his Marian Encyclical are telling us also that in today's world it is a necessity to focus much more than we have been doing on Mary's spiritual presence with us on earth. By viewing her in heaven, in a certain way she can be seen as being on God's side in distinction to being on our side, on earth. This does not mean opposite sides. Being on God's side means making Mary more the object of our prayers, sacrifices and devotions while being on our side means making Mary more a part of ourselves and everything we do. Does this lessen the mediation of Mary with Jesus in any way? Actually, it not only does not lessen it but it increases the power of this mediation. The power of her prayers is increased being on our side because her close presence increases the power of our prayers. Our prayer united with hers takes on increased value because our prayer, due to a closer union with Mary, now becomes her prayer.

Even though she is most certainly in heaven, physically and spiritually, she is also spiritually present with us on earth. She was on our side on Calvary when she became the Mother of the Church and the Spiritual Mother of the human race. (Jn 19:25, 26) She was on our side at Pentecost when in the midst of the Apostles and others, she exercised her role as Mother of the Church and also as exemplar for all of the disciples of Jesus. (Acts 1:14, 2:1-4) To focus more on Mary as being on our side could help to avoid problems that might develop for some in their relationship with Mary and Jesus. It could help to avoid the risk for some of seeing Mary as the dispenser of graces, gifts and favors without fully realizing that the source of all these is Jesus. It could also help to avoid the way of thinking that we can't approach Jesus directly or that we must have Mary in-between our relationship with Jesus. This does not mean that Mary is not always with us in our relationship with Jesus. She **is** always with us, beside us and even **within** us, urging us on to a closer union with Him and helping us with her presence and her prayers. This is especially true in our relationship with Jesus in the Eucharist, in our reception of Him in Holy Communion and in our visits with Him in the Blessed Sacrament.

The Presence of Mary brings the Presence of Jesus

Why should we want Mary to become more present beside us and within us? The reason is so that Jesus will become more present in our lives. St. Louis de Montfort, in his work, **True Devotion to Mary**, tells us that God wishes that His Holy Mother should be more known, more loved and more honored than she has ever been.[9] The reason for this is so that Jesus will be more known, more loved and more honored than He has ever been. The Fathers of the Church affirmed in the Vatican II document, **On the Sacred Liturgy**, that there is an inseparable bond between Jesus and Mary.[10]   In other words, wherever Mary is, Jesus will be there also. St. Louis also indicates, "The more He (the Holy Spirit) finds Mary, the more active and powerful He becomes in producing Jesus".[11]   He states further that "union with Jesus always follows necessarily on our union with Mary".[12]

It is true then, that the more Mary is present in our lives, the more Jesus will be present.

Consecration to Jesus through Mary

Pope John Paul II, in **Mother of the Redeemer**, mentions only St. Louis de Montfort, specifically, among the many teachers and witnesses of Marian spirituality. Our Holy Father recommends St. Louis' spiritual method of Consecration to Jesus Christ through a total entrustment of ourselves to Mary as an "effective means for Christians to live faithfully their baptismal commitments".[13] St. Louis urges us to bring about the presence of Mary more and more into our daily lives, to bring her into every aspect of our lives and most especially to bring her into our interior, spiritual lives. If we do, we are assured that we will find ourselves more closely united with Jesus. We will find that Jesus is becoming more and more the center of our lives.

My personal relationship with the spiritual method of St. Louis de Montfort goes back to December 8, 1949, when I first made this Consecration. I had experienced a religious conversion about one to two years before this while a student in college. I have attempted to put into practice this Consecration since then and can state without a doubt that it has been a powerful force in my life in keeping me centered on Jesus Christ and in preserving and making fruitful that original conversion experience.

Pope John Paul II has indicated that he has practiced and lived St. Louis' method of Consecration since his youth. Blessed Mother Teresa also practiced and lived this Consecration. The holiness of the lives of these two Christian witnesses is self evident.

Could the Church or the world have stronger witnesses to the effectiveness of this method of Christian spirituality than these two followers of Jesus Christ? They demonstrate how Mary's presence today in the world can be used to benefit in the most effective way the spiritual lives of the individuals who live this method and the spiritual lives of countless others.

NOTES

1. John Paul II, MOTHER OF THE REDEEMER, Encyclical, March 25, 1987, 1
2. Ibid., 28
3. Ibid., 32
4. Internet, www.Google.com, MARY PAGE, #4, The Blessed Virgin Mary Page, Marian Links, THE APPARITIONS OF THE VIRGIN MARY IN THE 20th CENTURY
5. Ibid., MARY PAGE, #4, The Blessed Virgin Mary Page
6. Dr. Mark Miravalle, S.T. D., THE DOGMA AND THE TRIUMPH, Queenship Publishing Company, Santa Barbara CA, 1998, Ch.3, p.100
7. op.cit., MOTHER OF THE REDEEMER, 47
8. Vatican II Document, ON THE CHURCH, November 21, 1964, 68
9. St. Louis de Montfort, TRUE DEVOTION TO MARY, Tan Books, Rockford, Ill.,1985, 55
10. Vatican II Document, ON THE SACRED LITURGY, December 4, 1963, 103
11. op.cit., TRUE DEVOTION TO MARY, 20
12. Ibid., 259
13. op.cit., MOTHER OF THE REDEEMER, 48

CHAPTER II

THE TRIUMPH OF THE IMMACULATE HEART OF MARY

The apparitions and messages of the Blessed Virgin Mary at Fatima, in the country of Portugal, in 1917, are of monumental significance for the world because they directly relate to God's most important work, the salvation of souls. The Catholic Church has confirmed the belief in the apparitions and messages as having come from God, Himself, many times since 1917. In our own time, the visits of Popes Paul VI and John Paul II to that place of heavenly visitation along with the Beatification of two of the visionaries on May 13, 2000, Francisco and Jacinta Marto, have firmly fixed that belief. Belief in Fatima is not presented by the Church as an article of faith but the messages are presented as something which can be believed in without any fear of doctrinal error. No new doctrines were revealed by Mary but the existence of hell was confirmed and what was new was the knowledge that souls were actually being lost in hell, apparently on a constant basis and apparently not a few in number but many. Mary, on August 19, 1917, put it this way, "---for many souls go to hell because they have no one to sacrifice and pray for them" [1]

Also revealed by the Mother of God were many messages in the form of prophecy. These messages included the knowledge that reparation was needed by God for the numerous sins by which He was offended and that God wanted reparation also to be made to the Immaculate Heart of Mary for the sins of humanity against that Heart. If people do what she asked, Mary said, then many souls would be saved and there would be peace. She also said, "The war (World War I) is going to end but if they (people) do not stop offending God, another and worse one will break out in the reign of Pius XI. When you see a night illuminated by an unknown light, know that it is the great sign that God gives you that He is going to punish the world for its crimes by means of war, of hunger, and of persecution of the Church and of the Holy Father. To prevent this, I come to ask the consecration of Russia to my Immaculate Heart and the Communion of reparation on the first Saturdays. If they listen to my requests, Russia will be converted and there will be peace. If not, she will scatter her errors throughout the world, provoking wars and persecution of the Church. The good will be martyred, the Holy Father will have much to suffer, various nations will be annihilated. In the end **my Immaculate Heart will triumph,** the Holy Father will consecrate Russia to me, and it will be converted and a certain period of peace will be granted to the world". [2] All of the messages and visions were confirmed on October 13, 1917, at the last apparition, by the famous 'Miracle of the Sun' which was witnessed by 70,000 people at the site of the apparitions and which Mary said would convince people that these events had truly been sent by God.

Reparation to the Immaculate Heart of Mary

Mary revealed at Fatima that her Immaculate Heart was an object of sin and that reparation needed to be made for all of the sins of humanity committed against her Heart. Mary had to have been an object of derision and hate when she stood beneath the cross. As her Son was mocked and scorned, so too, she had to have received similar treatment. This had been prophesied by Simeon when Jesus was a baby and being presented in the temple by His parents, "--and you yourself a sword will pierce so that the thoughts of many hearts may be revealed" (Lk 2:35) Although Mary was an object of sin on Calvary, how can she be an object of sin otherwise?

Pope John Paul II said that every sin has repercussions on the entire ecclesial body and the whole human family.[3] Every sin is an offense against God which could be described as a vertical element but also every sin involves an offense against humanity which could be described as a horizontal element. If Mary is an object of sin, she has to be involved in some way in this horizontal element. Since she is the spiritual Mother of the human race and every human person is her spiritual child, then it seems reasonable that she would have to be affected in some out of the ordinary way by the sins of her children.

Actually, since all of us are brothers and sisters in the human race, this horizontal element has to affect each of us also in some way. When we sin, especially against each other, we ought to be motivated to make reparation to each other. Reparation to the Heart of Mary then, has to be similar to reparation to each other. But this reparation, although similar, has to be of a much higher degree since her place as our spiritual Mother and as the Mother of God requires it.

Mary spoke further of reparation to her Heart when she appeared in a separate vision to Sister Lucia eight years after the Fatima visions. She said, " Look, my daughter, at my Heart surrounded with the thorns with which ungrateful men wound it with their blasphemies and iniquities. You, at least, try to console me, and announce that I promise to assist at the hour of death with the graces necessary for salvation, all those who on the first Saturdays of five consecutive months, confess, receive Holy Communion, recite part of my Rosary and keep me company for a quarter of an hour, meditating on its mysteries with the intention of offering me reparation".[4]

Only a Divine Person could atone for offenses against God, the vertical element, and this Jesus did, fully and completely. But for the horizontal element, the offenses against humanity, a human person, conceivably, could enter into this atonement. Pope John Paul II described it this way, "In her (Mary), the many and intense sufferings were amassed in such an interconnected way that they were not only a proof of her unshakeable faith, but also a contribution to the Redemption of all….It was on Calvary that Mary's suffering, beside the suffering of Jesus, reached an intensity which can hardly be imagined from a human point of view, but which was mysteriously and supernaturally fruitful for the Redemption of the world. Her ascent of Calvary and standing at the foot of the cross together with the beloved disciple were a special sort of sharing in the redeeming death of her Son."[5]

In the Gospel of St. John, Jesus, when told by Mary at the wedding feast that the bridal couple had run out of wine, addressed her with these mysterious words, "Woman, how does your concern affect me? My hour has not yet come". (Jn 2:4) According to the reflection of St. Louis de Montfort, this was not a rebuff at all but a silent invitation to the Heart of Mary from the Heart of Jesus to participate fully in the salvation of mankind. Would she open her Heart completely to whatever suffering Jesus might ask of her when His hour would come?[6] She indicated her yes to this invitation by telling the servants, "Do whatever he tells you". (Jn 2:5)[7] And on Calvary, Jesus, when His hour had come, from the cross, addressed Mary, again not as Mother but as, "Woman, behold your son". (Jn 19:26) Then He said to St. John, who represented the Church and the human race, "Behold, your mother", (Jn 19:27) making Mary the Spiritual Mother of every human person and especially the Church. After this, St. John tells us that "the disciple took her into his home". (Jn19:27)

This was Jesus' hour of triumph and the Woman was made an integral part in that triumph. This is the triumph that St. Paul tells of, "Death is swallowed up in victory. Where, O death, is your victory? But thanks be to God for giving us the victory through Our Lord, Jesus Christ". (1Cor 15:55,57) Mary participated in this triumph by opening her Heart completely to the unspeakable suffering asked of her, joining with Jesus fully and completely in His work of salvation. She would become intimately associated with Jesus' victory over Satan to the extent that she was given the power to decisively defeat the evil one, to crush his head and so Jesus' triumph, the triumph of His Sacred Heart, would become also the triumph of her Immaculate Heart. This was the fulfillment of God's prophecy to Satan in the garden of Eden, after the original sin, that the Woman and Satan would be enemies and that the seed of the Woman and thus the Woman, herself, would, in effect, crush the head of Satan. (Gen 3:15)

Jesus, through St. Margaret Mary, in the 17th century, made it clear that reparation is needed to the Sacred Heart of Jesus for all the sins of mankind committed against that Heart. And now we have God, in the 20th century, telling us, through His Blessed Mother and transmitted through three children that reparation is also needed to the Immaculate Heart of Mary for all of the sins committed against that Heart. Reparation has been made by God to be a needed part of the triumph of the Immaculate Heart of Mary and the Sacred Heart of Jesus.

Expression of the Triumph

How is this triumph of the Immaculate Heart of Mary to be expressed today in the time in which we live in accordance with the fulfillment of Mary's prophecy at Fatima? It is this author's belief that the triumph of the Immaculate Heart of Mary would seem to have to include at least three elements, **1. the elimination of the 'culture of death' and legalized abortion, 2. bringing peace and unity to a suffering and divided Church and to an** ailing, materialistic and generally pagan humanity, and the greatest triumph, 3. causing Jesus to shine forth in the hearts and souls of her children.

1. When Mary appeared in 1531, in Mexico, to Juan Diego, a converted Aztec Indian, the Aztec people were still, for the most part, practicing their pagan religion. The central part of this religion was human sacrifice and most particularly, child sacrifice. The culture of the Aztecs was advanced in many ways, including their judicial and legislative systems, science and the fine arts and architecture.[8] It is indicated by historians that the number of humans sacrificed was about 50,000 per year and that one out of every five children in Mexico was sacrificed.[9] From these appearances, Mary is known as Our Lady of Guadalupe, which seems to be a Spanish adaptation of the Aztec name with which she identified herself. After the Bishop was convinced that these appearances were, in reality from God, mostly because of the miraculous image of Mary which was left on Juan Diego's cloak, he gave permission for a church to be built at the site of the apparitions.

Mary had requested that a church be built so that her Son, Jesus, could be manifested to the people in order that "the sorrows, hardships and sufferings of the people could be alleviated and healed."[10] Within seven years after the apparitions, eight million Aztec and other Indians converted to Christianity and joined the Catholic Church.[11] The practice of human sacrifice was completely eliminated from the Aztec culture. The significance of the Virgin Mary appearing as a pregnant woman was not lost on the Indian peoples. She was bringing to this 'culture of death', to a people who were honoring death over life, Jesus, who was Life, itself, and Life triumphed over death.

In the United States, since Roe-Wade in 1973, it is estimated that well over 47 million innocent, unborn children have been killed through surgical abortions, not counting the early abortions caused by abortifacient birth-control pills. The non-violent, pro-life movement has been a powerful force in combating legalized abortion and the promoters of death. The Catholic arm of this movement has relied heavily on the praying of the Rosary along with a presence at the abortion mills to influence mothers not to get an abortion, to close abortion mills and to prevent them from being opened.

In Buffalo, N.Y., a focal point for the national pro-life movement in 1992, there were six free standing abortion mills. Now, over 15 years later, there are two. Since that time, surgical abortions have either been discontinued or markedly reduced at some area hospitals. The Rosary ministry of prayer and presence at the abortion mills has been a powerful factor in reducing the 'culture of death' in this area. The same kind of positive effect is true for many other areas in the United States and other countries where the 'people of life' have gathered together at abortion mills to pray the Rosary.

When the Rosary is prayed, the presence of Mary is brought to that place because the Rosary is the prayer of Mary, herself. It is Mary praying through that person. Since Mary becomes present, Jesus also becomes present because Jesus and Mary are always united. It is the presence of Jesus, who is Life itself, then, who overcomes the death and killing of abortion as it was Jesus who overcame the death and killing of human sacrifice in Mexico.

It is mainly the approval of legalized abortion that gives the strongest marking to the 'culture of death' today. Abortion can be said to be the **icon** of the 'culture of death'. It is not only in the United States but in almost every country in the world that abortion is legalized. Our present world is a 'culture of death'. Since the advent of legalized abortion in North and South America, Mary, as Our Lady of Guadalupe, has been designated as the "Patroness of Life for the Americas". As Mary brought the 'culture of life' to Mexico in 1531, she can bring the 'culture of life' to the entire United States as well to the other countries of the Americas and of the world. From a practical standpoint it would appear that the United States should be the first country to concentrate on since the United States is looked upon as a leader by many other countries. When the United States eliminates abortion, then many other countries will be influenced to follow suit. But this has to depend on the willingness of the children of Mary to bring Mary and thus Jesus to the United States, to the other countries of the Americas and to the world.

2. As the spiritual mother of the human family and of the Church, Mary, has been designated by God, through the power of the Holy Spirit, to achieve peace by drawing her children around herself, first to unite the family of the Church, then to unite the entire human family. It is the mother of the family who generally brings peace to the family by bringing the children together around herself. The mother of the family has to be made present so that the children can gather around her. This is done in a singularly and most effective way by praying the Rosary. The Rosary is, in reality, the prayer of Mary, herself. It is Mary praying through, with and in, those who pray the Rosary. When the Rosary is prayed, Mary becomes spiritually present in a powerful way. Why are Mary's prayers so powerful? It is because they are so pure and correspond so completely to the Will of Jesus.

By praying the Rosary more and more and praying it well, Mary is being proclaimed as the Mother of God more and more by the many Hail Marys which are being said. This will bring about a greater realization that Jesus is really and truly God, Himself, and dispose the children of the Mother to accept the fullness of the Gospel message which is a message of peace, love and truth.

Mary will bring peace and unity to the Church by drawing her children to the Eucharistic Sacrifice of her Son, Jesus, in the Mass, and in Eucharistic adoration. The Mass is the highest form of prayer possible because it makes present the one Sacrifice of Jesus on the Cross and gives Mary's children the opportunity to unite their hearts with the Heart of Jesus and His one Sacrifice.

When Jesus is made present in His Body and Blood, Soul and Divinity in the Eucharist, Mary also becomes present, not in her body but in a spiritual manner. Mary, in her spiritual presence, urges her children to give their lives over completely to her Son, Jesus. It is through union with Jesus in the Eucharist that the children of the Church are united, all by the power of the Holy Spirit.

It was Blessed Mother Teresa who said, many times over, that the greatest destroyer of peace in the world is abortion because it is war against the child.. When abortion is seen to be the destructive force that it is, not only on the innocent, pre-born children who are killed, but on the mother's themselves, and on families and others, then the people will rise up and eliminate this horror, not only in the United States but in every country in the world. Peace can only proceed from justice. This greatest of injustices, abortion, must be eliminated for peace to reign on the earth.

3. How, then is Jesus to shine forth in the souls of Mary's children? Mary indicated in the Fatima messages that her Immaculate Heart was an object of sin and that reparation needed to be made for all the sins and offences committed against the Immaculate Heart of Mary. Also indicated was Mary's statement that God wished to establish in the world devotion to her Immaculate Heart. This devotion to her Immaculate Heart was to include not only using her Heart as an object by asking for her intercession and making reparation but using her heart as an active instrument with which to love God and others. Popes Pius XII and John Paul II have both spoken to this latter form of devotion to the Heart of Mary. Pius XII said this, "Our devotion to Mary's Immaculate Heart expresses our reverence for her maternal compassion, both for Jesus and for all of us, her spiritual children, as she stood beneath the cross". John Paul II states a similar thought, "Mary's Heart, the Heart of both a virgin and a mother, has gone out to all that Christ has embraced and continues to embrace with inexhaustible love". This way of looking at devotion to Mary's Heart makes her Heart not an object but a subject and Jesus and her children become the objects of the love of her Heart. Mary's Heart becomes then, an active instrument in the life of the Christian for loving God and for loving others.

The practice of St. Louis de Montfort's method of complete entrustment to the Heart of Mary as a sure, quick and very effective way to give one's self completely to the Heart of Jesus, along with the practice of using Mary's Heart as developed in the reported messages to Father Gobbi of the Marian Movement of Priests, is the way that will cause Jesus to shine forth in the souls of her children. In a message to Father Gobbi on December 19, 1973, Mary is reported to have said, "When Satan will think himself the sure victor, he will find himself empty-handed and in the end the victory will be exclusively my Son's and mine. To win the battle I want to give you a weapon, prayer---offer yourselves to me so that I, myself, may always pray and intercede with my Son for the salvation of the world". And on October 13, 1917, this message was reported to have been received, "---the greatest victory of my motherly and Immaculate Heart will be to cause Jesus to shine forth in the souls of all my children". The greatest triumph of the Immaculate Heart of Mary will consist then, in the formation of Jesus in the souls of priests and the faithful in general. This formation of Jesus will be brought about by the action of Mary under the guidance and power of the Holy Spirit. But the triumph of the Immaculate Heart of Mary will only happen when enough of her children entrust and consecrate themselves to the Hearts of Mary and Jesus and then live that entrustment and consecration totally and completely.

NOTES

1. William Thomas Walsh, **OUR LADY OF FATIMA**, Doubleday, New York, N.Y., 1954, p. 120
2. Ibid., pp 81,82
3. John Paul II, **RECONCILIATION AND PENANCE,** Address, Dec. 2, 1984
4. op.cit., **OUR LADY OF FATIMA,** p. 219
5. Pope John Paul II, Apostolic Letter, **Salvifici Doloris**, n. 25
6. This was the fruit of St. Louis' meditation on the mystery of Cana.
7. Google: Meditation on the Words of Jesus, "My Hour has not yet come", #23, January, February Issue feature three 2003, Apostolic Letter **Rosarium Virginis Mariae,** 2003: Year of the Rosary, Five New Mysteries by Bro. Charles Madden, ofm, conv "Whenever Jesus spoke of His hour it always referred to his future Passion and Death Mary's prompt response directed at the waiters, "Do whatever he tells you", has been traditionally interpreted to indicate Mary's acceptance of Jesus' future Passion."
8. **A HANDBOOK ON GUADALUPE,** Park Press, Waite Park, MN, 2001, pp. 27-31
9. Ibid., p.139
10. Ibid. p. 10
11. Ibid., p. 218

CHAPTER
III

THE IMMACULATE HEART OF MARY
AND THE
SALVATION OF SOULS

The salvation of souls and the establishment of the Kingdom of God upon earth comprise the primary purpose of the Church upon earth.[1] On August 19, 1917, at Fatima, Portugal, during a series of apparitions from May to October, to three Portuguese children, it was revealed by God through the Blessed Virgin Mary, that "many souls were going to hell because there was no one to pray and make sacrifices for them".[2] In the previous month, on July 13, Mary had shown the children a vision of hell and the actual entry of souls going there. They were extremely frightened at this vision but were inspired and greatly motivated to become personally involved in order to prevent souls from going to hell. They had been asked by Mary at the first apparition on May 13, "Are you willing to offer yourselves to God and bear all the sufferings He will send you as an act of reparation for the sins by which He is offended and of supplication for the conversion of sinners?" Their immediate answer was, "Yes, we are". Mary then told them, "Then you are going to have much to suffer, but the grace of God will be your comfort".[3] After the children were shown the vision of hell on July 13, Mary told them, "You see hell where the souls of poor sinners go. To save them God wishes to establish in the world devotion to my Immaculate Heart.---".[4] Since this is God's desire, and God does not desire any way to do things but the most effective way, then devotion to the Immaculate Heart of Mary has to be the most effective way to save souls.

What is devotion to the Immaculate Heart of Mary?

Pope John Paul II says that it is the entrusting of a Christian as a child to its mother and then welcoming the mother into the interior of his or her Christian life.[5] It was from the cross that Jesus gave the Church and the human race a Spiritual Mother as he said to the Apostle John, "Behold, your mother. And from that hour the disciple took her into his home". (Jn 19:27) When John took Mary into his home, it was a figure of taking her into the interior of his Christian life and by so doing, entrusting his life to her. John becomes then for us an excellent 'model of entrustment'. When a Christian makes this entrustment, it is meant to be a total entrustment and involves giving to the Mother everything a person possesses. The Mother understands perfectly that this giving is truly meant to be an absolute giving to her Son. She then passes on to the Son the entire gift of the person's life but clothes the gift with herself so that it becomes her gift as well. And the Son regards the gift as not only coming from the Mother but sees only the Mother.

The gift then becomes a total entrustment to Mary and a total Consecration to Jesus Christ through the hands of Mary and with the Heart of Mary.

This is the method which St. Louis de Montfort proposes and Pope John Paul II recommends as the way for the Christian to give his or her life to Jesus Christ. He terms it as an "effective means for Christians to live faithfully their baptismal commitments".[6] St. Louis, in his treatise, *True Devotion to Mary*, teaches that all things should be done in union with Mary. In short, all of our thoughts, words and actions are united with the Heart of Mary and given to her as well as the value of all of our thoughts, words and actions past, present and future. By entrusting them to her they, in truth, become her thoughts, words and actions. And so, all of these things which are produced become covered over with the purity of her intentions, her wholeheartedness, her faith, her hope and her love. We should remember that John Paul II practiced this devotion since his youth and that Blessed Mother Teresa also followed this method.

Reported Messages from Mary

In a series of reported interior locutions, from 1973 to 1997, to the Italian priest, Father Stefano Gobbi, the founder of the Marian Movement of Priests, devotion to the Immaculate Heart is more completely developed. This development is in complete accord with Catholic teaching and has been considered as a compendium of the Fatima message and of the Marian doctrine of St. Louis de Montfort as well as the way of Spiritual Childhood of St. Therese of the Child Jesus.[7] The messages are essentially that we use the

Heart of Mary in everything we do, in all of our thoughts, words and actions and especially in our prayer. In the message of July 9, 1973, Mary said, "Learn to let yourself be possessed by me so that in everything you do it will be I who do it through you. It is so necessary now that it be the Mother who acts; and I want to act through you".[8] And in the message of July 21, 1973, Mary said, "To be consecrated to me means to let yourself be led by me. It means to entrust yourself to me, like a child who lets itself be led by its mother".[9] In a message directly related to the salvation of souls, Mary said on August 13, 1982, "Today, I say: how many souls you can save from the fire of hell and lead to paradise if, together with me, you pray and sacrifice each day for them".[10] And on October 13, 1982, Mary delivered this message to Father Gobbi while he was at Fatima, "How many souls there are, in fact, who go each day to hell, because the request I made of you, in this very place, to return to God along the road of prayer, penance and of interior conversion, has not been acted on".[11] And in the message of May 8, 1997, Mary said, "Through it (message of Fatima), I have asked for the consecration to my Immaculate Heart, as a sure means of obtaining conversion of heart and of life, and of leading humanity back along the road of its full return to God--so that the message of Fatima might come to its complete fulfillment.--These prophecies of mine are being fulfilled above all in this Pope of mine, John Paul the Second, who is the masterpiece formed in my Immaculate Heart".[12]

Why is devotion to the Immaculate Heart so effective for the salvation of souls?

The more and better this devotion is put into practice, the more that Mary, herself, will actually be entering into the battle for the salvation of souls. Mary draws on the mercy of Jesus in a special way since **she is full of mercy.** This does not mean that she is more merciful than Jesus because she draws her mercy from the infinitely merciful Heart of Jesus. But it means that the Mother of the King knows how to approach the King so as to touch the immeasurable mercy in His Heart and not to offend His justice in any way. The King wants to be approached in this way. He wants someone to ask from His all merciful Heart for pardon especially for those who are in danger of losing their souls. The person who most effectively can do this is Mary.

Devotion to the Immaculate Heart of Mary also produces in the soul that entrusts itself to her a strong desire to evangelize. Mary was the first Christian evangelizer. She brought the Word of God to her cousin, Elizabeth, not only in her body but in her words as well, mentioning the mercy of God. She proclaimed that "His mercy is from age to age to those who fear him" and "He has helped Israel, his servant, remembering his mercy…"(Lk 1:50, 54, 55)

The person who entrusts himself or herself to Mary and lives that entrustment will have Mary in the interior of that person's life. It is a spiritual truth that wherever Mary is present, Jesus is present also. They are never separated. Wherever the Holy Spirit sees Mary present in a soul, He immediately brings Jesus. The more that Mary becomes present, the more that Jesus will become present.[13] Indeed, the spirit of Mary is the spirit of Jesus.[14] The more a person lives out this entrustment to Mary, the more inspired that person will be to bring Jesus to others. Mary was inspired to bring Jesus to her cousin, Elizabeth, and as a result John the Baptist was sanctified in Elizabeth's womb. John was baptized by the Holy Spirit in the womb and set on the road of salvation from that point in time.

Even though Mary always brings Jesus with her, it is His mercy which is shown especially in this bringing because Mary is particularly able to draw on the infinite mercy of the Heart of Jesus. It is mercy that most especially is able to attract souls to conversion which places that soul on the road of salvation. When a person is filled with Mary, then that person is filled with Jesus, but especially filled with the mercy of Jesus because of the strong presence of Mary in that person. This is why total entrustment to the Immaculate Heart of Mary which results in a total Consecration to the Heart of Jesus is so effective for the salvation of souls. It is because Divine Mercy is, as it were, untapped from that Sacred Heart by the action of the evangelizer's heart united with the Immaculate Heart. The more that person's heart is united with Mary's Heart, then the more powerful will be the effect for the salvation of souls.

Who can be saved?

It is important for us to know as much as we can about who can be saved so that not only our prayers and sacrifices are offered to God but that we can do as much as possible to make the Gospel message known and loved. We do not know where on earth the souls are located, that Mary referred to, which are being lost or are in danger of being lost, but we can do as much as we can within our own sphere of influence to proclaim that Gospel.

The Catholic Catechism tells us that "believing in Jesus Christ and in the One who sent him for our salvation is necessary for obtaining that salvation".[15] This, however, does not mean that a person has to have an explicit faith in Jesus Christ to be saved. The Catechism also states that "Those who, through no fault of their own, do not know the Gospel of Christ or his Church, but who nevertheless seek God with a sincere heart and, moved by grace, try in their actions to do his will as they know it through the dictates of their conscience-those too may achieve eternal salvation".[16] St. Paul, in his Letter to the Romans states very clearly that the demands of the law are written on the heart of even the pagans. This means that every one who has not had the advantage of the Revelation to the Jews (the Ten Commandments) or the Christian Revelation will be judged according to the way in which that person has followed his or her conscience in obeying that law. (Rom 2:14-15) This law is called the natural law and it is written on the heart of every human person.[17] Essentially the Ten Commandments are equivalent to the natural law and can be said also to be "engraved by God in the human heart".[18]

Every single person on earth, therefore, is capable of being saved with no exceptions. The knowledge that souls can be saved without an explicit belief in Jesus Christ should not cause us to be complacent in any way. In fact, it should cause us to be more zealous in our concern for missionary activity to our own immediate world and to the whole world in general. When the extent of natural law violations such as contraception, abortion, fornication, adultery, masturbation and homosexual behavior as well as in-vitro fertilization, artificial insemination and the like is seen on a world wide basis, it is very easy to see how the tenets of the natural law, which are in every human being's conscience and depend for their interpretation on the use of right reason, can be obscured and the human will, essentially free, can go astray.

The Jews had an advantage over the rest of the human race before Christ because God gave them the Old Testament and set out for them explicitly the precepts of the natural law, the Ten Commandments. The Christian has an advantage over the non-Christian because of having the Word of God in the Old and New Testaments and because having faith in Jesus Christ makes many graces available to the follower of Jesus Christ which are not available to others. But the Catholic has a great advantage over everyone because the fullness of the Gospel message is made available to the Catholic person as well as the means to achieve salvation through the Sacraments and the surety that authentic Catholic teaching is the actual teaching of Jesus Christ. But salvation is not guaranteed to the Catholic or other Christians or to anyone because no one is different from St. Paul who said that even his salvation was not a certainty, "No, I drive my body and train it, for fear that, after having preached to others, I, myself, should be disqualified". (1Cor 9:27)

The obvious response to the Fatima revelation that many souls are being lost in hell is to do what Mary has requested of us, to pray and make sacrifices for those souls who are in danger of being lost. God always does things most efficiently and effectively. In the battle for human souls, God has provided the Church with the most efficient and effective way to save souls and that is **through total Consecration to the Heart of Jesus through a complete and permanent entrustment to the Immaculate Heart of Mary.** The Catholic Church's main purpose is the salvation of souls and the establishment of the Kingdom of God upon earth.[19] Individual Catholics, in particular, should be implementing the words of Mary at Fatima. Mary, perfectly reflecting the Heart of Jesus, is deeply and profoundly concerned about her children that are being lost forever and she is earnestly and urgently pleading with us, her children on earth, to assist her in this battle for the souls of her children. **How can we not respond to our Mother's heartfelt plea?**

NOTES

1. Vatican II Document, **THE CHURCH IN THE MODERN WORLD,** Dec.7,1965,45
2. William Thomas Walsh, **OUR LADY OF FATIMA,** Doubleday, New York, N.Y., 1954, p.120
3. Ibid., p.52
4. Ibid., p.81
5. John Paul II**, MOTHER OF THE REDEEMER,** Encyclical, March 25, 1987, 45
6. Ibid., 48
7. Father Stefano Gobbi, **TO THE PRIESTS OUR LADY'S BELOVED SONS,** The Marian Movement of Priests, St. Francis, Maine, Feb. 2, 1998, Preface, p.xxxv
8. Ibid., THE MOVEMENT IS NOW BORN, 1973, July 9, 1973, p.5, 3c
9. Ibid., July 21, 1973, 6a
10. Ibid., August 13, 1982, 249i
11. Ibid., October 13, 1982, 252d
12. Ibid., May 8, 1997, 594j
13. St. Louis de Montfort, **TRUE DEVOTION TO MARY,** Tan Books, Rockford, ILL, 1985,20
14. Ibid., 259
15. **CATECHISM OF THE CATHOLIC CHURCH,** Liguori Publications, Liguori, MO, 1994, 161
16. Ibid., 847
17. Ibid., 1954
18. Ibid., 2072
19. op.cit. **THE CHURCH IN THE MODERN WORLD,** 45

CHAPTER
IV

THE IMMACULATE HEART OF MARY
AND THE
DEFEAT OF SATAN

The Woman and the Garden of Eden

The triumph of the Immaculate Heart of Mary was foretold at the beginnings of the human race in the Garden of Eden after the original sin. It was God who said to the serpent after that sin, "I will put enmity between you and the woman, and between your offspring and hers. He will strike at your head, while you strike at his heel". (Gn 3:15) The identity of the Woman has been interpreted on different levels but the Church, consistently, on one of the levels, has seen the Woman to be Mary. She has been seen as crushing the head of the serpent, and thus defeating completely and decisively, Satan, the devil, by the power of her Son, Jesus Christ. She would be the means used by God to achieve this triumph.

The Nature of Original Sin

The original sin was essentially a sin of disobedience and

involved both of our first parents.[1] But even though it was a sin of disobedience primarily, it still may have involved other elements that are significant for our own times, today. Would it have been possible for the sexual powers to have been involved in this sin? God created the first man and woman in the state of original justice in which both had a true harmony where the soul's spiritual faculties had control over the body.[2] This is why, for example, the original sin could not have been a sin of lust. But this does not mean that the sexual powers could not have been involved in some way in this sin.

God had ordered Adam, "You are free to eat of any of the trees in the garden except the tree of knowledge of good and bad. From that tree you shall not eat; the moment you eat from it you are surely doomed to die." (Gn 2:16, 17)

It is the serpent who starts the dialogue. He asks the woman, Eve, "Did God really tell you not to eat from any of the trees in the garden?" The woman answered the serpent: "We may eat of the fruit of the trees in the garden; it is only about the fruit of the tree in the middle of the garden that God said, 'You shall not eat it nor even touch it, lest you die.' But the serpent said to the woman: "You certainly will not die! No, God knows well that the moment you eat of it your eyes will be opened and you will be like gods, who know what is good and what is bad." (Gn 3:1-5)

Genesis tells us that Eve ate of the fruit first, seeming to suggest that chronologically Eve may have committed this sin first and then Adam, instead of both of them together. But supposing this sin involved the loss of the sexual seed from the man? Supposing both of them had observed in the animal kingdom how life was transmitted, through passage of the seed of the male to the female. In their original state of creation and innocence, Adam and Eve were not subject to death, although they might not have realized this fully. So they might have reasoned, after the suggestion of the serpent, that God was trying to prevent them from gaining the secret of life and also His Wisdom and becoming like Him by forbidding them to eat of the fruit of this particular tree. They could also have reasoned that if God was trying to prevent them from obtaining these secrets, then He was keeping them from something to which they were entitled, by their nature, which was to be like God, Himself. This was what Lucifer had wanted, to be like God, Himself. So they listened to the serpent because they wanted to be like God, Himself.

The irony of all this is that God fully intended to give them eternal life and all of His wisdom which they could possibly want according to their nature but in order to do this they would have to simply admit that God possessed everything by His very nature as Creator, absolutely, and that they, in fact, as creatures, possessed nothing, absolutely. In addition, they would have to believe that God would not order them to do something which was not for their good. But they believed, as Lucifer did, that they were entitled to be like God simply because of their nature. They did not realize that to obtain eternal life and to obtain God's Wisdom they had to admit that God was who He was by nature and therefore was due by themselves and all of creation complete and total submission and self-giving.

After creating them and blessing them, God had given this command to both the man and the woman, "Be fruitful, multiply--" (Gn 1:28)   But instead of following God's command, they chose to follow the serpent's advice. The seed of Adam could have been seen as the fruit of the tree which they were forbidden by God to eat or even to touch. They knew that the seed of the male was of vital importance to them because it was through the seed that life was transmitted. But through the serpent's suggestion, they could have thought that God was trying to keep them from their true destiny which was to be like God. They could have intentionally then opposed God's command which was for their own good and procured the seed of the male for the purpose of ingesting the seed and thus, as they thought, giving them the secret of life and the Wisdom of God and making them like Him. By purposely procuring the seed of the male for a purpose other than that which God had commanded, they touched and ate of the fruit of the tree of the knowledge of good and bad. As a result, their death was immediate as God had foretold but it was a spiritual death, the death that comes through mortal sin resulting in separation from God. Their physical death would now come for them also and not only for them but also for all of their descendants, the entire human race.

Satan had lied to them, but they believed him. The devil had influenced Adam and Eve to commit the original sin by doing the same thing he had done, wanting to be like God in His Wisdom and then acting on that belief. Lucifer knew that he couldn't be exactly like God but whatever it was that God was commanding him to do at the time of his test, he refused to do. Perhaps it was submitting himself eventually to the God-man, Jesus Christ, to whom submission and obedience would have to be given or possibly it could have been that God showed Lucifer a vision of the God-man and the Woman, to whom all angels would have to demonstrate submission and obedience. This may help to explain why the serpent approached the woman first whom he may have considered to be the most prone to temptation. If this was the woman to whom God wanted him to show submission, then he would attack her and try and bring about her downfall. In so doing, he would show God what a mistake He had made.

But God surprised the serpent and mysteriously indicated to him that hostilities would continue between the Woman and himself and between her seed and his seed. And that in the end the serpent would be totally defeated by the Woman and her children. Satan, because of his wrongful pride in his angelic nature, would not consider putting himself in a posture of submission to even someone like a God-man, and certainly not to a creature such as this woman if that comprised the angels' test. His sin was a sin of pride and disobedience. He was saying, in effect, no one has the right to tell me what to do and what not to do, not even God. Satan convinced Adam and Eve that no one had the right to tell them what to do and what not to do, not even God. They committed essentially the same sin as Lucifer had, which was a sin of pride and disobedience. Their sin, in addition, could very possibly have involved the use of the sexual powers.

Immediately after the events in the garden, the Scriptures tell us that they obeyed God's command , "Be fruitful, multiply---" (Gn 1:28) and used their sexual powers for sexual intercourse as God intended, "The man had intercourse with his wife, Eve, and she conceived and gave birth to Cain". (Gn 4:1) They now used their sexual powers as God had commanded them but the damage had already been done in terms of their original innocence. Now even the observation of their naked bodies became a problem. They knew something was wrong and then they hid themselves. What had been a source of glory for them, their uncovered bodies, now became a source of shame.

Contraception, a Universal Sin.

Contraception, which is a common form of the intentional loss of the seed, is extensively used in just about every country in the world today. If the original sin did involve the sin of intentionally losing the seed of the male, the original sin is then blanketing the world today because of this extensive use. Contraception is used to intentionally block the conception of a child. It is a refusal to obey God's command, as expressed in the natural law and written into the heart of every human being that every act of sexual intercourse (marriage or conjugal act) between husband and wife should be open to the transmission of human life.[3]

The practice of contraception sets the stage for the practice of abortion. Pope John Paul II mentioned many times that in those places where contraception is freely practiced, abortion thrives. Legalized abortion is now accepted in the great majority of countries on earth. Statistics confirm the Holy Father's statement that there is a direct relationship between the use of contraception and the growth of abortion giving the lie to the argument that contraception reduces abortion.

The same elements that were possibly present in the original sin, the intentional loss of the seed of the male along with the idea that God doesn't have the right to tell me what to do or what not to do, are present today in the widespread use of contraception resulting in the worldwide legalization of abortion. In a certain sense, the world is reliving the original sin not just by pride and disobedience but also by the serious misuse of the sexual faculties.

The effects of the original sin had a devastating effect on our first parents and the entire world and a similar situation exists in the world today with so much pride and disobedience and the world-wide serious misuse of the sexual faculties. This includes not only contraception but widespread homosexual behavior and fornication including couples living together before marriage. There has been a general justification promoted by much of the media in recent years of fornication in general, homosexual behavior, contraception and even masturbation. These behaviors have at times even been justified by some Catholic theologians. Fortunately, this has been clarified by the Encyclical of Pope John Paul II, ***The Splendor of Truth, (Veritatis Splendor),*** and the **Catholic Catechism** which state unequivocally that contraception, abortion, fornication, and masturbation along with artificial insemination, in-vitro fertilization and the like, are all intrinsically evil and therefore immoral under all circumstances.[4] Since such extensive contraception and fornication are resulting in that greatest of injustices, legalized abortion, can we not expect that this will have a terrible effect on the world again?

At Fatima, in 1917, during World War I, Mary prophesied that unless people stopped sinning, God was going to punish the world and that another world war would occur. As we know, this war did occur with horrible effects for the entire world. Other terrible effects were also prophesied including the persecution of the Holy Father and the Church.

All of these prophecies were conditional and depended on whether the people of the world would stop sinning. But Mary said that no matter what happened, in the end, her Immaculate Heart would triumph and a period of peace would be granted to the world. And so we have this assurance from God that victory is guaranteed as it was guaranteed after the original sin that the head of the serpent would be crushed (Gn 3:15) and that the Woman would be instrumental in this victory.

The Triumph of Women Over Satan in the Old Covenant

There were women, among the chosen people, who would pre-figure the triumph of the Blessed Virgin Mary over Satan and were used by God to achieve His purposes, as evidenced in Holy Scripture, which was a type of victory over Satan.

Rebecca, the wife of Isaac, arranged for her younger son, Jacob, to receive his father's blessing rather than Esau, the older son. Isaac's blessing included that nations would serve Jacob and peoples would bow down before him. (Gn 27:29) It was from the descendant of one of Jacob's sons that Jesus would eventually be born.

Deborah, the prophetess, and a judge in Israel, told the Israelites the exact day to attack the enemy, that the enemy would be defeated, and that the Lord would deliver the general of the King's army into the hands of a woman. (Jg 4:6-9) This woman, **Jael,** would crush the head of the general. In her canticle, after the victory, Deborah sang, "Blessed among women be Jael." (Jg 5:24)

Hannah was childless and poured forth her soul to the Lord to grant her a male child whom she vowed to consecrate to the Lord. Her prayer was granted and when the child was weaned, she dedicated him to the Lord and left him in the temple with those who cared for him. (1Sam. 1:24) This child was Samuel, the prophet, who later would be responsible for the enthronement of King David. It was from the line of King David that Jesus would be born. Hannah proclaimed her prayer of praise and thanksgiving and in that prayer she says, "---I have swallowed up my enemies, I rejoice in my victory". (1Sam 2:1) Her prayer bears several points of resemblance to the prayer of Mary, who while bearing the Son of God in her womb, greeted her cousin, Elizabeth, with her prayer of praise and thanksgiving. (Lk 1:46-55) Mary had to have been familiar with Hannah's prayer and most probably was able to meditate on it while traveling to visit her cousin, Elizabeth, after the visitation of the angel, Gabriel.

Judith, with great faith and courage, went alone into the camp of the enemy when the Jewish people had given up hope because of the power and strength of their enemy, the Assyrians, and their commander, Holofernes. She returned with the head of Holofernes and was greatly acclaimed by the people for saving them from destruction. They praised her in this way, "--You are the glory of Jerusalem! --You are the highest honor of our race!" (Jdt 15:9)   The Church has applied these acclamations to Mary in her sacred liturgy. It was also said of Judith, "May you be blessed by the Lord Almighty forever and ever!" (Jdt 15:10)   Mary, herself, would prophesy, in her prayer of praise and thanksgiving, upon visiting her cousin, Elizabeth, "--behold, from now on will all ages call me blessed". (Lk 1:48)

Queen Esther, as a representative of her people, the Jews, at the risk of her life, presented herself to the king to intercede for her people to prevent them from being destroyed. She was given the power by the king to gain a victory over these enemies and save her people. The number 13 plays a role here because it was on the 13th day of the 12th month that the Jewish people were saved and on which they destroyed their enemies.

Ruth, the Moabitess, although not a Jew, exemplifying faith, loyalty and love, chose to worship the one, true God and became the mother of Jesse, the father of David, from whom Mary descended and thus Jesus.

All of these women showed forth exceptional faith, love and courage in pre-figuring Mary as the Woman who would triumph over the enemy, Satan.

Cana, Eden and Calvary

In the Gospel of St. John, Jesus, when told by Mary that the couple had run out of wine at the marriage feast, addressed her not as mother but with these mysterious words, "Woman, how does your concern affect me? My hour has not yet come". (Jn.

2:4) This seeming rebuff was not so, as St. Louis de Montfort tells us. It was, in his view, a silent invitation from the Heart of Jesus to the Heart of Mary to participate fully in the salvation of mankind when His hour would come, which would be the hour of His passion and death.

Mary indicated her "yes" to this invitation by telling the servants, "Do whatever He tells you". (Jn. 2:5) The fact that Jesus worked the first of his many miracles here to satisfy her request demonstrates that He was truly pleased with His mother's response and on Calvary, from the cross, just before He died, Jesus addressed Mary, again not as mother, but with the following, "Woman, behold your son". And to John He said, "Son, behold your mother". (Jn. 19:6) The Woman, by reason of her cooperation with Jesus in His redemptive action and the total opening of her Heart to Him to whatever He asked for, was declared by Him to be the Spiritual Mother of not only John but of the Church and indeed of the entire human race. This was Jesus' hour of triumph and the Woman was used by Jesus as an instrument in that triumph.

This is the triumph that St. Paul tells of, "Death is swallowed up in victory. Where, O death is your victory?---But thanks be to God who gives us the victory through Our Lord. Jesus Christ". (1Cor. 15:54,55,57) Mary participated in this triumph by opening her heart completely to whatever suffering was asked of her in God's plan of salvation as she stood beneath the cross on Calvary. He made the victory of His Heart the victory of her Heart also. She was God's instrument in the complete and decisive defeat of Satan. This was the triumph that God had indicated in the Garden of Eden would take place by the Woman being given the power to crush the head of Satan and completely defeat him.

Simeon's prophecy to Mary, when Jesus, as a baby, would be presented in the temple, according to Jewish law, would be realized underneath the cross, "Behold, this child is destined for the fall and rise of many in Israel, and to be a sign that will be contradicted and you, yourself, a sword will pierce so that the thoughts of many hearts will be revealed". (Lk. 2:34,35) What is this sword? It has to be the sins of the human race visited against the Heart of its Mother which caused such unspeakable suffering and had such a devastating effect on the Heart of the Spiritual Mother.

Pentecost

As the early Fathers of the Church taught, the Church was born from the side of Christ when, on the cross, "--- one soldier thrust his lance into his side and immediately blood and water flowed out." (Jn 19:34)

The manifestation of the birth occurred on Pentecost Sunday when the Church was assembled around Mary praying earnestly for the coming of the Holy Spirit. The Holy Spirit came on the Heart of the Mother first and from that Heart proceeded to fill each of those assembled in the upper room, the Cenacle, as it says in Holy Scripture, "They were all filled with the Holy Spirit---". (Ac 2:4)

This was reminiscent of the conception of Jesus by the Holy Spirit in Mary's womb. It is generally believed that Mary was pouring forth prayer for the coming of the Messiah when she received a visitation from the angel, Gabriel. But it is safe to assume that the Anawim (the remnant of believing Jews) were also praying for the coming of the Messiah. It was her prayers combined with the prayers of the believers that brought Gabriel for this confrontation that would shake the foundations of the world. With Mary's "yes" (fiat) came the Holy Spirit and the conception of the Son of God in the womb of the Virgin Mother. And now at Pentecost it is Mary praying again, this time as Mother and this time in the midst of her believing children, for the coming of the Holy Spirit. She prays as a disciple of her Son, Jesus, and as the Spiritual Mother of her special children, the Church.

The result of these prayers was amazing. Peter, the head of the Church, and the others, were filled with courage and inflamed with zeal for preaching the Gospel message. About three thousand people were converted that day and the disunity that began at the tower of Babel was now overcome. God's remarkable triumph was provided again through the Woman who continued to give herself unreservedly to the Divine Will.

Fatima and the Number 13

It is not without great significance that Mary appeared to the three children at Fatima in Portugal in 1917 on the 13th day of each month. The only exception to this was when she appeared on the 15th of August because the children were confined in jail on the 13th. It is the Woman throwing down the challenge to Satan that his days are numbered and that his total defeat is now imminent. She knows that this will certainly provide motivation for him to work that much harder but this is all part of her plan to raise up strong and courageous children in these latter times.

The number 13, down through the centuries, has represented Satan's attempt to mimic God and the Holy Trinity, 10 being the number of perfection and 3 the number of the Trinity. In the Book of Genesis (14:4), a rebellion took place in the 13th year. The number 13 has been associated with rebellion, apostasy, defection, corruption, disintegration and revolution. Many superstitions cluster around the number 13. Satan has an unholy trinity, himself, the anti-christ and the false beast. The beast rising out of the sea occurs in the Book of Revelation, Chapter 13. Thirteen has been a satanic number because when the moon is full, the Satanists and pagans have celebrated Black Sabbath and each celebration includes a Black Master and 12 coven members, exactly to mimic Jesus and the 12 Apostles. Every year has 13 such occasions, every 28 days. The number 13 has been considered by many to be under the control of Satan and his minions and therefore unlucky and a number to avoid. This is why the 13th floor has been eliminated from high buildings and the number 13 from hospital rooms.[5]

The assassination attempt on the life of Pope John Paul II occurred on May 13, 1984. The Pope saw this entire incident as under the complete control of the Blessed Virgin Mary and that somehow she saved his life. It is precisely because this number has been considered to be Satan's number that Mary chose to appear on this day of the month. She threw down the gauntlet, as it were, to the evil one, and she was telling him that his total defeat was near. It was also to show the people of the world that she has been given the power not only over this number but over Satan, himself. Mary has been telling the world since Fatima that Satan is on his way to complete and utter defeat and that although this defeat would be accomplished by the power of God, it would be through the instrumentality of her Immaculate Heart. The Woman was taking the initiative in the battle for human souls. As foretold in the Book of Genesis, the head of the serpent would now be crushed and his time was short.

The Woman has been given the power to defeat Satan but she must find the way to transmit this power to her children. The emphasis is not so much on the overcoming of Satan as it is on the salvation of souls. This is the heart of the warfare. The triumph that Mary wants to achieve is in the hearts and souls of her children. The war is waged within the heart and soul of each one of her children and Satan is making an all out effort to gain the souls of as many of her children as he can.

The Woman and Her Children

The Woman appears again in the Book of Revelation, "Now a great sign appeared in the sky, a woman clothed with the sun, with the moon under her feet, and on her head a crown of twelve stars." (Rv 12:1)   Satan and the fallen angels also enter the picture here, "Then another sign appeared in the sky; it was a huge, red dragon---. Its tail swept away a third of the stars from sky and hurled them down to the earth". (Rv 12:3,4) Then Satan pursues the Woman and her children, "Then the dragon became angry with the woman and went off to declare war on the rest of her offspring". (Rv 12:17)

The war that the children of the Woman are engaged in with Satan will go on until the children are given the power to overcome him. How is this power to be transmitted to the children? Enough of her children have to open their hearts totally and completely and give themselves over to her by means of a total entrustment and giving to her Immaculate Heart for this to happen. Again it will be the Mother who gains the triumph through the power of her Son but this time it will be the Mother acting through her children which will provide the victory. Love and mercy bound together with faith and courage will provide the victory and the humiliation will be that much greater for Satan because it will be at the hands of her and those whom he considers so much inferior to himself.

NOTES

1. **CATECHISM OF THE CATHOLIC CHURCH,** Liguori
   Publications, Liguori, MO,1994, 397, 390
2. Ibid., 400
3. Ibid., 2366
4. Ibid., 2357, 2376, 2377
5. Internet, Google, **Fatima and the Number 13,** #2, *The Pattern and the Prophecy,* E.W. Bullinger, Kriegel Publications, c, 1967, p.205

CHAPTER
V

THE COMING OF MARY -
THE COMING OF JESUS

The primary purpose of the Catholic Church is the salvation of souls and the establishment of the Kingdom of God upon earth.[1] We pray for this establishing every time we pray the Lord's Prayer, the prayer that Jesus taught us, ---**Thy kingdom come, Thy will be done, on earth as it is in heaven.--- (Mt 6:10)** It is certain that Jesus will come again, then will follow the Last Judgment. But will Jesus come again in glory to earth apart from this final coming? According to a statement given by Cardinal Ratzinger in 1990 in answer to a question addressed to the Congregation for the Doctrine of the Faith about this subject, the answer was, "The Church has never taken an official stand on this subject, one can interpret either way". It is possible then, at the present time, to believe as a faithful Catholic that there will be some type of intermediate coming before the final coming and the Last Judgment.[2]

Intermediate Coming?

Several Fathers of the Church did believe that there would be a middle or intermediate coming of Jesus to earth, among whom were St. Justin Martyr, St. Irenaeus, St. Hippolytus, St. Augustine, and St. Bernard of Clairvaux. St. Bernard, in his ***Sermo 5, Adventu Domini***, clearly speaks of another coming of Christ which he places between the first coming (in the flesh, at his birth) and the final coming (in the flesh, for the Last Judgment). This intermediate coming, he says, will be invisible, not in the flesh, while the other two are visible, i.e., in the flesh.[3]

This belief in an intermediate coming of Jesus is not millenarianism which has been condemned by the Catholic Church. Millenarianism is the belief that Jesus Christ will come down from heaven to earth and reign with His saints for a literal, one thousand years in the flesh (glorified body). St. Bernard says that the "intermediate coming is a hidden one; in it only the elect will see the Lord within their own selves, and they are saved in this middle coming, He is our rest and consolation".[4] St. Bernard seems to be relating that in this intermediate coming, those, who are living on earth at that time will be assured of their eternal salvation. ("and they are saved") It could be stated that his meaning is only that of the coming of Christ in word and sacrament in the present time. But then, if so, why does he say that "they are saved"?

In relation to this, the Blessed Virgin Mary said at Fatima that in the end her Immaculate Heart would triumph and that a "certain period of peace would be granted to the world". We do not know for certain what this period of peace means. Does it mean that those who would be living at that time would be living in a type of paradise on earth and that their salvation would be assured? The answer to this is not known. What we do know for certain are Mary's expressions about the need for devotion and reparation to her Immaculate Heart and prayers and sacrifices for the salvation of souls.

The doctrine of the Millennium, also known as the temporal or millenary kingdom and described as an "age to come" an "era of peace" or "some mighty triumph of Christianity before the end", as distinguished from Millenarianism or mitigated Millenarianism, has been accepted as sound doctrine. This belief states that Jesus will come in glory, but in His spirit and not in the flesh, and that He will reign in our hearts (wills) and will reign in a most powerful way by means of the Eucharist. The duration of this Kingdom does not have to be interpreted as a literal, one thousand years.

A work known as ***The Teaching of the Catholic Church, A Summary of Catholic Doctrine, (edited by Father George D. Smith)*** which bears the Church's required seals and was published in 1952 by a theological commission of qualified experts, clearly states that it is not against Catholic teaching to believe or profess "a hope in some mighty triumph of Christ here on earth before the final consummation of all things. Such an occurrence is not excluded, is not impossible; it is not at all certain that there will not be a prolonged period of triumphant Christianity before the end".[5]

Pope John Paul II has referred to a "new springtime in Christianity" which will be intensely Eucharistic and at its dawn will "make Christ the heart of the world".[6] In a talk given in Rome on March 30, 1985, he said, "The Church is the community of the little ones - of the little children who await the return of Jesus in glory - " At the end of a speech given in Edmonton, Canada, on September 17, 1984, the Holy Father said, "---May justice and peace kiss once again at the end of the second millennium, which is preparing us for Christ's coming in glory". On August 15, 1993, in a homily given in Denver, at world Youth Day, he concluded his remarks with: "This pilgrimage must continue---it must continue in our lives; it must continue in the life of the Church as she looks to the Third Christian Millennium. It must continue as a new advent, a moment of hope and expectation until the return of the Lord in glory. Your celebration of this World Youth Day has been a pause along the journey, a moment of prayer and of refreshment, but our journey must take us on even further, even to the return of the Lord in glory!"[7]

At Fatima, in 1917, Mary said that if people did not stop sinning, the world was going to be punished by another and more terrible war, by hunger, persecution of the Church and of the Holy Father, but that **in the end her Immaculate Heart would triumph and a certain period of peace would be granted to the world.** In the interior locutions given to Father Stefano Gobbi, the founder of the Marian Movement of Priests, Mary is reported to have said that "---the triumph will be realized through a new birth of Jesus in hearts and souls". and that "the triumph of my Immaculate Heart cannot come in all its fullness, until I have brought them all to my Son, Jesus".[8]

In addition to Mary's foretelling, Popes John XXIII, Paul VI and John Paul II all have spoken about a Second Pentecost to come. The First Pentecost took place in the cenacle in Jerusalem and all there were transformed and "filled with the Holy Spirit". (Acts 2:4). But the second will take place on a worldwide scale. It will transform the hearts and souls of all and all will be filled with the Holy Spirit. This Second Pentecost to come will very likely coincide with the Triumph of the Immaculate Heart of Mary, the Eucharistic Reign of Jesus and the period of peace foretold by Mary at Fatima. It will be the fulfillment of the Lord's Prayer, **"...Thy Kingdom come, thy will be done on earth as it is in heaven..."** (Mt 6:10) How then, is the world to be prepared for this coming of Jesus?

Preparation for the Coming

According to St. Louis de Montfort, in order to prepare for the coming of Jesus, Mary must come first. As Mary was the way that Jesus came to earth the first time, so too, Mary must be the way for all subsequent comings. St. Louis may not have foreseen this intermediate coming of Jesus but the principles he sets down for the final coming of Jesus have to be true for any coming of Jesus.[9] He does say, however, that "towards the end of time,---God will raise up great men (ones), full of the Holy Ghost and imbued with the spirit of Mary, through whom this powerful Sovereign will work great wonders in the world, so as to destroy sin and establish the Kingdom of Jesus Christ, her Son, upon the ruins of this corrupt world".[10]

In the first coming, it was the prayer of Mary, herself, together with the prayers of the Anawim (the remnant or small group of believing Jews) that caused the Father to send the Angel Gabriel to her for the answer which would result in the Redeemer coming to earth. Along with the Anawim, Mary was praying for the coming of the Messiah, not for herself as mother, because as St. Augustine tells us, she had already taken a vow of virginity. Because of the force of her prayers and the eminence of her virtues, God could not resist her.[11] It must be admitted that the prayers of the Anawim, who were anticipating the coming of the Messiah, were necessary also but it was the prayer of Mary that turned the tide and brought the Angel to earth for the confrontation which was to shake the very foundations of the universe. Mary's Fiat ("let what you have said be done to me".) (Lk1:38) was the crucial decision which would set in motion the plan of salvation for the human race.

How is the coming of Mary to be effected? Mary, herself, gives us the answer to this. At Fatima, Mary said that God wished that devotion to her Immaculate Heart be established on the earth so that souls could be saved. John Paul II has indicated that devotion to the Immaculate Heart of Mary is in reality, a total entrustment or giving to the Heart of Mary. This entrustment must be a complete and total giving to Mary who will then give everything we have given her, in Consecration to Jesus. Along with the giving, the entrustment and consequent Consecration must be lived totally and completely. This is the spiritual method of St. Louis de Montfort which John Paul II is urging the members of the Church to put into practice.[12]

For Mary to come upon the earth, it must be a spiritual coming. She must be brought into the very interior life of the Christian. Mary must become present in the soul in a powerful way, so powerful that Mary's life becomes its life.   Mary's life must be established in the soul so that it is no longer the soul that lives but Mary living in it.[13] St. Paul proclaimed, about 23 years after his conversion experience, "---I live, no longer I, but Christ lives in me." (Gal 2:20)   This life of Mary is not the same as the Life of Jesus in the soul because the Life of Jesus is indeed, Life itself, from whom all life proceeds, including the life of Mary. Jesus said, "I am the Way, the Truth and the Life". (Jn 14:6) The life of Mary living within us is similar to that by which we live in each other in the Mystical Body of Christ. However, Mary's life is much more powerful and produces remarkable fruits. This is because whenever the Holy Spirit finds the life of Mary, He produces immediately the Life of Jesus. So that whenever we fully live the Consecration to Jesus Christ by entrusting ourselves totally and completely to the Heart of Mary we can say, "I live, no longer I, but Mary lives in me." And when we can say that, we can also say with St. Paul, "I live, no longer I, but Christ lives in me".

How do we effectively make Mary present in the interior of our Christian lives?

Most importantly, it is through our prayer. We must pray with the Heart of Mary. In our prayer we must ask the Holy Spirit to come and we can ask Him to come through the powerful intercession of the Immaculate Heart of Mary. It is not necessary to use words in our prayer. It is only necessary that we abandon ourselves to the Holy Spirit and ask Mary to pray within us with the prayer of her Heart. Our prayer may be a simple one of adoration and letting Mary adore the Father, Son and Holy Spirit living within us through sanctifying grace. But we must let Mary, through the power and guidance of the Holy Spirit, determine the mode of prayer, whether of adoration, petition, reparation, contrition, thanksgiving or praise.

In order to do this, it is necessary to set aside a certain period of time each day to be perfectly alone and persevere in this prayer, at least 20 minutes each day, but preferably 30 minutes to one hour. It is especially in preparation for the Mass that this prayer takes on its fullness because at the Mass we become identified with Mary at the time when the one Sacrifice of Jesus on the Cross is made present for us. Our reception of Jesus in Holy Communion becomes Mary's prayer and we give ourselves over to her and trust that she will welcome Jesus at that time in the manner she determines. This will be much better than if we determined this solely by ourselves.

Our prayer must be Mary's prayer and it must be the foundation of our entrustment and total giving to her. From this prayer will flow the giving of ourselves in our everyday lives. From it will flow an increased zeal for the salvation of souls. From it will flow a desire to make sacrifices in the seemingly small happenings in our lives. We will come to realize that these seemingly small events are in reality great opportunities to sacrifice for the salvation of souls.

From Mary praying in our souls will come the ability and the desire to use Mary's Heart in every circumstance of our lives. The

Heart of Mary will be performing every thought, word and action in our lives and will bring to mind and complete in us those omissions which we tend to neglect. All of this requires our continued total giving to Mary of ourselves and then submitting ourselves lovingly to her Heart acting within us.

With this presence of Mary will infallibly come the presence of Jesus. When Mary is present in enough hearts and souls then Jesus will come and establish His Kingdom on earth because He will not be able to resist the power of Mary's prayers which will be raised up through the hearts of her children. This intermediate coming **will not be a coming in the flesh but it will be an invisible coming and Jesus will reign in His Eucharistic presence.** It will be a kind of heaven on earth but it will not be arrived at without much suffering on the part of Mary's children and for some, martyrdom.

Mary has been urging us most powerfully since Fatima in 1917 to prepare ourselves for what is to come, for persecutions and tribulations that will precede the period of peace. The period of peace will be a time of great happiness and tranquility upon earth for those of her children on earth but it will be preceded by a period of great suffering and tribulation.

Mary tells us through her reported messages that Her Immaculate Heart is the safe refuge for any and all of her children.[14] She does not promise us to be free from suffering but she does promise us that we will be spiritually protected when we live within her Immaculate Heart. She wants us to use her Heart for everything we do, and this is all inclusive, for every thought, word and action of our lives. For Jesus to come, Mary must be present and the only way she can become present is through her children living totally this entrustment to her Immaculate Heart and consequent Consecration to the Sacred Heart of Jesus

But this total giving of ourselves to the Heart of Jesus through the Heart of Mary must be done soon! It must be done now! The salvation of many souls depends on how quickly and how soon we make this Consecration and entrustment and then live it totally.

How much do we love Jesus ?
How much do we love Mary ?
We need to prove it.

NOTES

1. Vatican II Document, **THE CHURCH IN THE MODERN WORLD**, 45.1
2. Rev. Albert Roux**, IN DEFENSE OF THE ORTHODOXY OF THE MARIAN MOVEMENT OF PRIESTS, OUR LADY'S MESSAGES AND FATHER GOBBI,** Marian Movement of Priests, St. Francis, Maine, March 3, 2001, pp.21,22
3. Ibid., pp. 14,15
4. Ibid., p. 15
5. Ibid., pp. 13,14
6. Ibid., p. 17
7. Ibid., pp. 18,19
8. Rev. Albert Roux, **THE TRIUMPH OF THE IMMACULATE HEART OF MARY** Booklet ,Marian Movement of Priests, St. Francis, Maine, Feb.22, 2001, pp. 4,5
9. St. Louis de Montfort, **THE SECRET OF MARY,** The Montfort Fathers, Bay Shore, NY, 1947, Revised Edition, 58
10. Ibid.,59
11. St. Louis de Montfort, **TRUE DEVOTION TO MARY,** Tan Books, Rockford, Ill, 1985, 16
12. John Paul II, **MOTHER OF THE REDEEMER,** Encyclical, March 25, 1987, 48
13. Op. cit., **THE SECRET OF MARY,** 55, St. Louis puts it this way, "This devotion (True Devotion to Mary), faithfully practiced, -establishes, even here below, Mary's life in the soul, so that it is no longer the soul that lives, but Mary living in it; for Mary's life becomes its life"
14. Father Stefano Gobbi, **TO THE PRIESTS, OUR LADY'S BELOVED SONS,** The Marian Movement of Priests, St. Francis, Maine, Dec.31, 1997, 604g,i

CHAPTER
VI

A METHOD OF CONSECRATION
TO THE
SACRED HEART OF JESUS
THROUGH
ENTRUSTMENT
TO THE
IMMACULATE HEART OF MARY

In order to facilitate the increase of the spiritual presence of the Immaculate Heart of Mary on earth, the following method as set forth in the next pages is presented with the hope that many Catholics will take the opportunity to enroll themselves as servants of Mary's Immaculate Heart.

Of course, there are other ways in which this Entrustment and Consecration can be accomplished. But this is believed to be a practical way to follow up on these Reflections which have been written to try and inspire Catholic people to offer their very selves for the purpose of making the Immaculate Heart of Mary and thus the Sacred Heart of Jesus, spiritually present on the earth on which we live.

If, after reading the following pages about the **Community of the Servants of the Immaculate Heart of Mary,** a person believes he or she can fulfill these Requirements and desires to enroll in this Community, then that person should make a suitable preparation by actually carrying out the Requirements as set forth for a prayerful, thirteen day period of reflection, namely: 1. Making and trying to live the daily Act of Consecration and Entrustment 2. Performing at least 20 minutes of daily mental prayer using the Immaculate Heart of Mary 3. The daily praying of at least five decades of the Holy Rosary, praying the Rosary with the Heart of Mary 4. The wearing of the Brown Scapular of Our Lady of Mount Carmel.

After a person has successfully completed this thirteen day trial period and believes that he or she can continue to fulfill these Requirements on a daily basis, then that person should select a date for beginning his or her membership. The Recommendations should be looked at also to determine if there are any that could be carried out at this time. Although not absolutely necessary, this date may, with much fruitfulness, be begun on a Feast Day of the Blessed Virgin Mary.

Once the responsibility is assumed, it is fervently hoped that the servant of the Immaculate Heart of Mary will persevere to the end of his or her life on this earth.

The person enrolling should send his or her name, address and e-mail address, if applicable, and the date of beginning membership to the following:

Center - Community of the Servants of
   the Immaculate Heart of Mary
P.O. Box 203
Hamburg, NY 14075
Attention: Director

CHAPTER
VII

THE COMMUNITY
OF
THE SERVANTS
OF
THE IMMACULATE HEART OF MARY

A. MEMBERSHIP

Membership in the Community as a servant is open to all Catholics, lay, religious or clergy.

B. CONDITIONS FOR MEMBERSHIP

A servant has to entrust one's self to the Immaculate Heart of Mary completely and totally. The servant has to give one's self to the Heart of Mary with nothing held back. The gift must include one's entire person, body and soul, whatever one is and has, whatever one will be and will have, and whatever one was and had. This gift will be for all time and for all eternity. The servant must ask Mary to give to the servant her Heart to use in every aspect of the servant's life. This entrustment will result in the complete and total giving in Consecration of the servant to the Sacred Heart of Jesus from the Immaculate Heart of Mary in the spirit of St. Louis de Montfort as taught by our Holy Father, Pope John Paul II, in his Papal Encyclical, **Redemptoris Mater (Mother of the Redeemer)**.

Mary always gives everything given to her to Jesus and never keeps anything for herself. This giving, however, will result in the servant still belonging to Mary as her child and if the servant is faithful will result in that person's residing in the Heart of Mary now and for all eternity. Since the Immaculate Heart of Mary always resides in the Sacred Heart of Jesus, then that child and servant of Mary will be in the Heart of Jesus now and for all eternity.

C. PURPOSE

The purpose of the Community is to make Mary and thus her Immaculate Heart spiritually present on earth and to achieve holiness for the individual servants. This is to be done by the total and complete Consecration of the servant to the Sacred Heart of Jesus through total and complete Entrustment to the Immaculate Heart of Mary and then living out that Consecration and Entrustment in one's life.

This purpose will help to bring about the salvation of souls and the establishment of the Kingdom of God upon earth which the Fathers of the Church indicated at Vatican II in the document, **Gaudium et Spes (The Church in the Modern World)** is the "single intention" of the Catholic Church. This can be furthered effectively by this Consecration and Entrustment. At Fatima in 1917, Mary said to the three Portuguese children that God wished to establish devotion to the Immaculate Heart of Mary upon earth and she related this to the salvation of souls. The servant of Mary must be completely devoted to the salvation of souls and must make every effort in his or her life to use Mary's Heart for this purpose.

St. Louis de Montfort teaches that as Mary preceded Jesus' first coming on earth, so too, she must precede all subsequent comings. The servant of Mary then makes Mary spiritually present on earth by making her spiritually present in the servant's heart by this Consecration and Entrustment and then living this out in everyday life. By this living out in a total and complete manner, the servant's heart, by using Mary's Heart in every thought , word and action, is taken over completely by Mary's Heart and in a real and spiritual sense becomes Mary herself. That servant can then say with all truth, "I live, no longer I, but Mary lives in me" and since Jesus and Mary are always united, then that servant can also say with St. Paul, "I live, no longer I, but Christ lives in me". (Gal 2:20)

When the presence of Mary becomes so powerful on earth, then Jesus will come and establish His Kingdom. The establishment of this Kingdom will not be the final coming but will be a "period of peace" which was foretold by Mary at Fatima. It will be an invisible coming and Jesus will rule by means of His Eucharistic presence. Pope John Paul II has referred to a "new springtime in Christianity" which will be intensely Eucharistic and at its dawn will "make Christ the heart of the world".

This coming will also coincide with the Triumph of the Immaculate Heart of Mary which Mary also foretold at Fatima.

She said that after a time of tribulation, her Immaculate Heart would triumph and then would come a "period of peace."

D. MEMBERSHIP REQUIREMENTS

1. The servant must promise to make the following Act of Consecration and Entrustment at the beginning of every single day of one's life and do the best that he or she can do to live this out every single day of one's life.

CONSECRATION to the
SACRED HEART of JESUS
through
ENTRUSTMENT to the
IMMACULATE HEART of MARY

O Mary, please give me your Immaculate Heart this day so that I may use your Heart in every aspect of my life. I give and entrust myself entirely and completely into your hands and your Immaculate Heart this day, all that I am and have, all that I ever will be and will have, and all that I ever was and had, to give entirely in Consecration to the Sacred Heart of Jesus Christ, my Lord and Savior, now and for all eternity.

2. The servant must each day promise to set aside at least 20 minutes each day, but preferably 30 minutes to one hour, for mental prayer. This prayer should involve the use of the Immaculate Heart of Mary and the servant should allow the Heart of Mary to pray in that person's interior in whatever way she chooses. This prayer

should begin by asking Mary to make this prayer the prayer of her Heart. The Holy Spirit should be invoked and may be done through the following prayer:

Come Holy Spirit, through the powerful intercession of the Immaculate Heart of Mary, your well beloved spouse!

This mental prayer may be a simple prayer of adoration of the Father, Son and Holy Spirit. It may also involve prayers of petition, reparation, thanksgiving, praise and contrition.

3.   The servant should promise to pray as a minimum five decades of the Holy Rosary of the Blessed Virgin Mary each and every day of one's life, preferably on the days designated by the Church for the Joyful, Luminous, Sorrowful and Glorious Mysteries with special attention given as to how the Immaculate Heart of Mary views and lives out each mystery. This means that the servant should pray the Rosary with the Heart of Mary. If at all possible, the servant should pray additional mysteries of the Rosary each day, even the twenty decades. The meditations of the Immaculate Heart mysteries of the Rosary may be used for this purpose.

4.   The servant should promise to wear always the Brown Scapular of Our Lady of Mount Carmel as a sign of belonging to her as her child and servant.

It is naturally assumed that the servant will be a faithful member of the Catholic Church, believing in the fullness of the teaching of

Jesus Christ, the Lord, as proclaimed by the Church He established to teach His truth in the world until the end of time. The servant will especially hold fast in his or her heart the teachings of the Catholic Church on the dignity and respect for human life in all its stages from conception to natural death with the prohibition of abortion and euthanasia as a central focus.

Failure to live up to any aspect of the promises made to be a member of the Community of the Servants of the Immaculate Heart of Mary is in no way binding under pain of sin. If a servant, after making a promise to make the Act of Consecration and Entrustment each day, fails to do this or any of the other Requirements set forth, then that servant can simply start anew each day to do one's very best in the future to carry out these Requirements.

E. RECOMMENDATIONS

1. The servant should try to attend the Eucharistic Sacrifice each day, if at all possible. At each Mass, the servant should especially keep in mind that the one Sacrifice of Jesus on the Cross is made present, sacramentally. The servant should ask Mary, especially at the time of Consecration, to unite his or her heart with the Heart of Mary and then ask Mary to offer these two hearts in union with the one Sacrifice of Jesus on the Cross, to our heavenly Father. At the time of Communion, the servant should especially ask Mary to receive Jesus with the prayer of her Heart. The member should allow Mary to honor Jesus in whatever way she chooses, be it of adoration or some other manner of prayer she might choose.

The servant should keep in mind that Jesus, in the Eucharist, is not a passive person but very active. He is continually involved in giving Himself in love totally in this Sacrament. The servant should be giving himself or herself totally in the same way to Jesus but always united with the Heart of Mary so that it is in reality the prayer and love of Mary's Heart that responds to the love of Jesus.

2. The servant should avail himself or herself of the Sacrament of Reconciliation on a frequent basis, monthly if possible, realizing that this Sacrament is a powerful way to make progress in the spiritual life.

3. It is recommended that the servant, according to one's state of life, if not already required, should pray the Liturgy of the Hours, also known as the Divine Office, the prayer of the Church. The priest and some religious are required to pray the entire Liturgy of the Hours each day. The deacon and many religious are required to say at least morning and evening prayer each day. The lay servant, if possible, should attempt to pray morning and evening prayer each day. The servant should be especially attentive, as at the Eucharistic Sacrifice, to pray the prayer of the Church with Mary's Heart. When a person prays the Liturgy of the Hours, that person is praying with the entire Church on a worldwide and universal basis. When Mary's Heart is used to pray this prayer, then the prayer takes on a much greater effectiveness because it becomes Mary's prayer, the prayer of the Mother of the Church.

4. The servant should attempt to make the reading of the Holy Scriptures a necessary part of his or her Christian life. The

Fathers of the Church at Vatican II urged all the Christian faithful "to learn the 'excelling knowledge of Jesus Christ' (Phil 3:8) by frequent reading of the divine Scriptures" for as St. Jerome has said, "Ignorance of the Scriptures is ignorance of Christ." Reading the Scriptures with Mary's Heart can be especially fruitful for one's spiritual growth because the Word of God can be seen then from Mary's unique and totally Christ centered perspective. Let the servant also remember what the Fathers of the Church stated at Vatican II, quoting St. Ambrose, "--that prayer should accompany the reading of Sacred Scripture---for we speak to Him when we pray; we hear Him when we read the divine saying."

5.   It is highly recommended that the servant read the excellent works of St. Louis de Montfort especially, **True Devotion to Mary**, and **The Secret of Mary**, and then to prepare for, make the Act of Consecration in the way set out by him and then to live it out in one's life. The Act of Consecration to the Sacred Heart of Jesus through Entrustment to the Immaculate Heart of Mary, which is prescribed as a daily requirement for the servant, although different in wording from St Louis' Act of Consecration as prescribed in his work, **True Devotion to Mary**, is not meant in any way to be a substitute for this Act. The difference in wording results from an effort to make the Act of Consecration and Entrustment more directly centered on the Immaculate Heart of Mary and to conform to the words of Mary at Fatima where she said that "God wishes to establish in the world devotion to her Immaculate Heart". It is also an effort to capture the spirit of St. Louis' Act of Consecration as recommended by Pope John Paul II

in his Encyclical, **Mother of the Redeemer**, for daily use by the servant and also focusing on the Immaculate Heart of Mary. It is in the making and living out this Act that the Holy Father states is an "effective means for Christians to live faithfully their baptismal commitments."

Also recommended very highly is the collection of reported messages from the Blessed Virgin Mary to Father Gobbi, from 1973-1997, entitled, **TO THE PRIESTS, OUR LADY'S BELOVED SONS,** (The Marian Movement of Priests, Rev. Albert Roux, P.O. Box 8, St. Francis Maine, 04774-0008), as these messages reveal an excellent way of developing devotion to the Immaculate Heart of Mary.

F. SPIRIT OF THE COMMUNITY

The spirit of the Community is that it will always be under the complete and total control of the Immaculate Heart of Mary. The servant understands that the gift of one's self to the Immaculate Heart of Mary is not absolute in the same strict sense as the giving of one's self absolutely to the Sacred Heart of Jesus since Jesus is a Divine Person. But since Mary has been designated as the Spiritual Mother of each and every human person, she has been given the right to hold each of her children who give and entrust themselves to her in a special way closely in her Heart. Since she is so closely united to Jesus, this enables her child to belong in an absolute manner to our Lord and Savior Jesus Christ while remaining intimately united to her Immaculate Heart.

The essence of the spirit of the Community is to identify totally and completely with the Immaculate Heart of Mary in one's entire life. It is to make Mary spiritually present on earth through the Consecration and Entrustment to the Heart of Jesus through the Heart of Mary.

Mary was the first evangelizer, and the spirit of the community also involves the evangelization of others to this method of making the Immaculate Heart of Mary spiritually present on earth, through personal contacts and witnessing, talks, homilies, articles in various kinds of publications and any way in which this consecration and entrustment can be spread to others, using whatever media means are available.

The most powerful means of evangelization will always be the example of the servant's life upon others as the Heart of Mary and thus the Heart of Jesus shines forth in the servant's life. As St. Francis of Assisi stated to one of his brothers as they were entering a town to evangelize, that they were going there to preach the Gospel and that sometimes they might use words.

What needs to be kept in the forefront of one's efforts at evangelization is that its effectiveness will always depend on prayer, and especially prayer before our Lord and Savior, Jesus Christ in the Eucharist. It is from Jesus in the Eucharist that all evangelization on earth finds its success.

Every servant should center his or her life on Jesus in the Eucharist because each one's life will in actuality be Mary's life and Mary on earth will always make Jesus the center of life on earth. This includes as much prayer as possible with Mary's Heart before the Heart of Jesus in the Blessed Sacrament and inclusion, if possible, in programs of perpetual adoration of Jesus in this Most Holy Sacrament.

May the Sacred Heart of Jesus Christ be praised in the Most Holy Eucharist now and until the end of time and may He be especially praised by the Immaculate Heart of Mary as she prays through the hearts of her children on earth!

G. DAILY MENTAL PRAYER

Daily mental prayer relates directly to the purpose of making Mary and thus her Immaculate Heart spiritually present on earth and to the servant pursuing holiness. The servant must totally identify with Mary and this can be effectively done through a concentrated effort by the servant to persevere in mental prayer on a daily basis. There are two factors that are necessary for this to happen. The first and most necessary is grace which is the basis of all true prayer. The other is the perseverance of the servant who must build up a discipline to strengthen this habit of praying with the Heart of Mary on a regular basis. With perseverance, the servant will dispose one's self to receive the gift of the awareness of Mary's presence in the soul. It must be emphasized that this is a gift; it cannot be achieved by one's own efforts alone and it may not be received by everyone. Yet St. Louis de Montfort, speaking of life in Mary, calls it (the awareness of Mary's presence), a particular grace of the Holy Spirit which the faithful "must merit"[1]; that is to say, they must dispose themselves for it.[2]

If persevered in, the manner of praying with the Heart of Mary becomes an habitual manner of praying. This will occur whether or not the servant receives the grace of the awareness of Mary's presence in the soul. This habitual manner of praying when combined with the living out of total giving of self to the Heart of Mary and thus to the Heart of Jesus, will allow Mary to take over the servant's life. The reason that this type of mental prayer, using Mary's Heart to pray, is emphasized so strongly is that if it is used effectively by enough people, and then lived completely, it will result in Mary, and thus her Immaculate Heart, becoming spiritually present on earth in a very significant way, and to establish in the one who prays in this manner, a continuing thirst for holiness, which relate directly to the twofold purpose of the Community of the Servants of the Immaculate Heart of Mary.

H. A POSSIBLE PROBLEM OF IDENTIFICATION WITH MARY FOR MEN

Some men may object to or consider it an obstacle to growth in the Christian life to identify with Mary who is the ultimate woman of the human race. Is the fact that Mary is a woman with her complete femininity going to interfere in some way with the masculinity of a man who wishes to identify with her? This is a reasonable question and needs to be given some attention.

Let us first consider Mary as the perfect model of the Church. She is presented by the Church as the ideal Christian, i.e., follower of Christ. From a spiritual standpoint, as to how to be a follower of Christ, she is the one every Christian should model themselves after, men and women. The imitation of Christ for a virtuous Christian life was practiced by His followers in His own time and since that time up to and including the present and should be continued to be practiced. By imitating Mary, it does not mean that a person does not imitate Jesus. In fact, the more and better a person imitates Mary, the more and better a person will be imitating Jesus.

When a man identifies with Mary, he does not identify with her feminine characteristics. He identifies with the movements of her Immaculate Heart which are always movements directed toward serving God in some way or serving her children of the human family. He retains his masculinity in every aspect of his life. St. Ambrose, back in the fourth century, put it this way; "Let the soul (heart) of Mary be in each of us (every Christian)---." The method of identification with Mary has been in the Church for many centuries. If practiced properly by men, this method can only lead to a greater identification with Jesus which is the purpose of the Christian life.

NOTES
1.   St. Louis de Montfort, **TRUE DEVOTION TO MARY,** Tan Books, Rockford, Ill., 1985, 258
2.   Emil Neubert, S.M., S.T.D., **LIFE OF UNION WITH MARY,** The Bruce Publishing Company, Milwaukee,WI, 1960, p.193

CHAPTER
VIII

ST. LOUIS DE MONTFORT'S
CONSECRATION

THE ACT OF CONSECRATION

Consecration to Jesus Christ,
the Incarnate Wisdom,
through the Blessed Virgin Mary

I, <u>Name</u> , *a faithless sinner, renew and ratify in thy hands, the vows of my Baptism; I renounce forever: Satan, his pomps, and works; and I give myself entirely to Jesus Christ, the Incarnate Wisdom, to carry my cross after Him all the days of my life, and to be more faithful to Him than I have ever been before.*

In the presence of the heavenly court I choose thee this day for my Mother and Mistress. I deliver and consecrate to thee as thy slave, my body and soul, my goods, both interior and exterior, and even the value of all my good actions, past, present and future; leaving to thee the entire and full right of disposing of me, and all that belongs to me, without exception, according to thy good pleasure, for the greater glory of God, in time and in eternity.

NOTES

1. Op. cit., St. Louis de Montfort, **TRUE DEVOTION TO MARY,** pp. 197-198.

    The Act of Consecration consists of about two additional pages of prayer addressed to Jesus and Mary. What is presented here is the heart of this Consecration.

CHAPTER IX

THE IMMACULATE HEART MYSTERIES OF THE ROSARY

The Immaculate Heart Joyful Mysteries of the Rosary

1. The Annunciation

The angel Gabriel appeared to the Virgin Mary and asked her if she would consent to be the mother of the Messiah. Mary had been praying for the coming of the Messiah but not for herself as mother. As St. Augustine tells us, she had already taken a vow of virginity and therefore questioned the angel as to how she could be a virgin and a mother at the same time. When she determined that the angel's message was from God, she responded with the complete opening of her Heart and a total yes.

Mary, we ask you to give us your Heart so that we may open our hearts completely and respond with a total yes to whatever it is that Jesus is asking of each one of us.

2. The Visitation

Mary, without hesitation, went to be with her cousin Elizabeth when she learned from the angel Gabriel that she was already in her sixth month of pregnancy. At the sound of Mary's greeting John the Baptist leaped for joy in his mother's womb. Mary considered the needs of Elizabeth first in preference to her own needs and was the first bearer of Jesus for others. Jesus' Heart was already beating and was united with the Heart of Mary when she proclaimed her prayer of praise and glory to God.

Mary, we ask you to give us your Heart so that we may think first of the needs of others in preference to our own and so that we may learn better each day how to be the bearer of Jesus for others.

3. The Nativity

Jesus was born in a cave in Bethlehem. The Creator of heaven and earth, from whom all created things have come, chose to be born surrounded by the barest of material goods. Mary and Joseph shared in this poverty and totally accepted the circumstances of Jesus' birth with joyful and open hearts. They welcomed the One who created all, to creation, itself.

Mary, we ask you to give us your Heart so that we may use material things only so that they will lead us to spiritual things and a greater love for Jesus and others.

4. The Presentation in the Temple

Joseph and Mary presented Jesus in the temple in obedience to Jewish law. Their Consecration of Jesus to the Father was a loving recognition of the Son belonging to the Father in an absolute manner and of the temporary custody which had been granted to them.

Mary, we present ourselves to you so that you may give us in Consecration to Jesus in loving recognition of our belonging to Him in an absolute manner while remaining your obedient children. Take us into your Heart and keep us there forever for then we shall with certainty be in the Heart of Jesus forever.

5. The Finding of the Child Jesus in the Temple

Mary and Joseph found Jesus in the temple after a heart rending search. The loss of Jesus for three days caused them great sorrow and pre-figured His death and burial in the tomb.[1] His finding pre-figured His Resurrection and the joy that would be experienced by Mary's Heart because of it. The person that sins mortally experiences the loss of Jesus in his or her soul. If that person repents, then they can experience the joy and peace that comes with finding Jesus.

Mary, we ask you to give us your Heart and your hatred of sin so that we may never experience the loss of Jesus. If we have the misfortune to do so, help us with the prayers of your Heart so that we may find Jesus again and His joy and peace through the Sacrament of Reconciliation.

NOTES
1. ***The Jerome Biblical Commentary,*** **The Gospel According To Luke**, Carroll Stuhlmueller, C.P., (II) 46.

The Immaculate Heart
Mysteries of Light of the Rosary

1. The Baptism of Jesus

Jesus was baptized by John the Baptist not because He needed to be but because it was God's plan that He was to be identified with sinners at the outset of His Mission. Was Mary, as a disciple of Jesus, present for the Baptism? The Scriptures do not tell us but we do know that Mary always exemplified the meaning of Baptism by opening her Heart completely to the Will of God in her life and then doing it, **wholeheartedly.**

Mary, we ask you to give us your open Heart, so that we, too, as disciples of Jesus, may participate fully in the way that God is calling each one of us in His plan of salvation for ourselves and for the human race.

2. The Wedding Feast at Cana

Mary came up to Jesus at the feast and said simply, "They have no wine". And Jesus said to her, "Woman, how does your concern affect me? My hour has not yet come". The title of "Woman" for Mary was again given when Mary would stand beneath the cross when Jesus' hour had come. (Jn 19:26) According to the reflections of St. Louis de Montfort, what Jesus said at Cana was accompanied by a silent invitation from the Heart of Jesus to the Heart of Mary to participate fully in His work of salvation and redemption when His hour would come. Mary answered yes to Jesus by telling the servants, "Do whatever He tells you". Jesus then proceeded to answer Mary's prayer and work the first of His many miracles by changing the water into wine.

Mary, we ask you to give us your Heart, so that we may never be afraid to approach the Heart of Jesus no matter what our need may be. Help us to believe with your Heart the truth of Jesus' statement, "---All things are possible for God". Help us to carry out in our own lives the message you gave to the servers but which is also meant for us, "Do whatever He tells you".

3. The Proclamation of the Coming of the Kingdom of God

At the beginning of the Gospel of Mark, Jesus says, "The Kingdom of God is at hand. Repent and believe in the Gospel". The proclamation of the coming of the Kingdom is accompanied by a call to conversion of life. These words express the very heart and soul of the Gospel message. The Fathers of the Church at Vatican II re-affirmed this statement of Jesus by stating that, by virtue of one's Baptism, **every** Christian is not only **called but obligated** to live a life of holiness. Jesus said this, "---You shall love the Lord, your God with **all** your heart, with **all** your soul and with **all** your mind. This is the greatest and first commandment. The second is like it. You shall love your neighbor as yourself". (Mt 22:37-39)

Mary, we ask you to give us your Heart, you who as the perfect disciple always gave everything to God in all that you did, never holding anything back. Help us, then to pursue holiness by using your Heart to live out these loving commands of Jesus, to love God completely and to love our neighbor as ourselves.

4. The Transfiguration

At the Transfiguration, the Divinity of Jesus is revealed. This is done so that Peter, James and John may be strengthened for the difficult times that would lie ahead, especially the passion and death of Jesus. They hear the voice of the Father telling them that Jesus is His beloved Son and that they must listen to Him.

Mary, please give us your Heart so that our belief in the Divinity of Jesus may always be strengthened. Help us to pray always, and to pray the Rosary well with the conviction and love of your Heart so that we may always be prepared for whatever may happen in our lives. Help us to use your Heart to always listen to the words of Jesus in Holy Scripture and put these words into practice in our own lives.

5. The Last Supper

Jesus, through the priest, makes present for us at the Mass, the Sacrifice of His passion and death. At the Mass, we are given the opportunity to unite ourselves and our lives with the one Sacrifice of Jesus on the Cross, made over two thousand years ago. The miracle is not only that the bread and wine are truly changed into the Body and Blood of Jesus but that also His one Sacrifice is made truly present. The Eucharist is "a sacrament of love, a sign of unity, a bond of charity, and a Paschal Banquet in which Jesus Christ is consumed, the mind is filled with grace and a pledge of future glory is given to us".[1]

Mary, we ask you to give us your Heart so that at the Mass we may be wholehearted in offering ourselves to our Heavenly Father in union with Jesus in His passion and death on the cross. Help us by the use of your Heart to prepare worthily for each Mass we attend and in Holy Communion to take some time to be alone with Him using your Heart. Help us to be a bond of charity and the bearer of Jesus to others and strengthen in us the belief and desire for future glory.

NOTES
1. Vatican II Document, *Constitution on the Sacred Liturgy, 47*

The Immaculate Heart Sorrowful Mysteries of the Rosary

1. The Agony in the Garden

Jesus suffered the bloody sweat in the garden at the terrible thought of our sins. The Apostles fell asleep on Him but Mary could not sleep, knowing in her Heart that Jesus was soon to be handed over to His death. She sensed in her Heart that something dreadful was happening to Him and she watched and waited in prayer. Mary sensed also that she, too, was an object of sin and that Jesus needed her cooperation in His work of salvation.

Mary, help us to realize and to feel with your Heart the meaning of sin in our own lives and of others. Give us your Heart so that we may have your hatred of sin and your desire to console the Heart of Jesus.

2. The Scourging at the Pillar

Mary was in the crowd outside the place where Jesus was scourged. She could not see what was happening but she could hear the sound of the lashes. Each sound of the lashes left a mark on her Heart. She felt in her Heart what Jesus felt in His body. She knew that this suffering of Jesus was to atone primarily for sins of the flesh and she knew that her purity and virginity were intimately associated with this suffering of Jesus.

Mary, give us your Heart so that we may love purity and chastity with your love and so bring consolation to the Heart of Jesus for all the sins of the flesh being committed in the world today.

3. The Crowning with Thorns

The crown of thorns was pushed cruelly into the head of Jesus causing Him grievous suffering. This was Satan's hour in this act of supreme mockery. Jesus was mocked as a false King as Satan had mocked God after the sin of Adam. These were acts of the highest pride. But Jesus overcame this pride of Satan and all the sins of pride ever committed by His unmatchable humility. Because of her profound humility, Mary opened her Heart completely to whatever suffering God asked of her. The great humility of her Heart helped to strengthen Jesus and helped Him to overcome these sins of pride.

Mary, give us your Heart so that we may be strengthened in humility and so that we may console the Heart of Jesus for all the sins of pride being committed in the world today.

4. Jesus Carries His Cross

Jesus embraced His Cross because it was the expression of his love for His Father and for every human person. He knew that He had to reach Calvary with His cross. He fell three times but He persevered in His journey and received help in carrying His cross from Simon of Cyrene. Mary, too, knew that Jesus had to reach Calvary. Each time He fell, her Heart suffered all the torments He felt in His body. When Jesus met Mary on the way to Calvary, He felt the strength and courage of her Heart and knew He could count on the perseverance of her Heart to help Him reach His goal.

Mary, give us your Heart so that we may persevere in our following of Jesus, to do His Will and whatever He asks of us in our walk with Him.

5. The Crucifixion and Death of Jesus

Jesus' Heart was filled with love for all men and for each individual person who had ever lived and who ever would live. This, in spite of the fact that He knew that some would reject His love and be lost forever. His love would never diminish, however. He looked down from the cross and saw His Mother, John, and the others, bravely standing with Him. It was especially the love He felt from His Mother's Heart that gave Him consolation and strength to help Him complete His Mission with the knowledge that she entered into His plan of salvation with a full and open Heart. Her Heart was crucified in spirit and she suffered a martyr's death in spirit. This was the fulfillment of Simeon's prophecy that a sword would pierce her Heart. Nothing can compare to the pain that Jesus suffered in body, mind and spirit but Mary entered into that suffering as much as a human person could enter into it. As a result, she became the spiritual Mother of the human race and especially of the Church, while being a helper to Jesus in His redeeming action.

Mary, give us your Heart so that we may love Jesus and everyone and everything He loves with the love of your Heart. Help us to give ourselves completely to Jesus as He gave Himself to each of us so that we may fully enter into His plan of salvation for ourselves and for all people.

The Immaculate Heart
Glorious Mysteries
of the Rosary

1. The Resurrection

Jesus rose from the dead on the third day after His passion and death. The Resurrection presents for us a mystery of faith. The fact that Jesus rose from the dead confirms our faith in His Divinity and His Mission. We believe not only in everything He said and did but also in His love for each one of us. Jesus' love for each of us will never fail us no matter what happens in our lives. The Scriptures do not tell us that Jesus appeared to His Mother first but several Doctors of the Church as well as St. Ignatius of Loyola believed that she was the first witness of the Resurrection.

It makes sense that Jesus would appear first to the one whose Heart never stopped believing in Him. Her Heart had to have been overcome with joy at His resurrected presence, the joy that always comes with persevering faith.

Mary, we ask you to give us your Heart so that we may never stop believing in Jesus, in everything He said and did and especially in His immeasurable love for each one of us. We ask that we may experience the joy of your Heart in finding the resurrected Jesus in all the circumstances of our lives.

2. The Ascension

Jesus ascended into heaven forty days after His Resurrection. The Ascension presents for us a mystery of hope. The supernatural virtue of hope is a desire to be in heaven with Jesus for all eternity. Hope overcomes all discouragement and even despair. The Heart of Mary, although tempted to discouragement, never stopped hoping and always expressed the utmost confidence in everything Jesus said and did. This nurtured and strengthened her desire to become more and more united with the Heart of Jesus. We need hope in our lives because we can be tempted to discouragement and to believe that we are not good enough to have a close, personal relationship with Jesus. The truth is that no matter who we are, Jesus wants this close, personal relationship.

Mary, give us your Heart so that we may never lose hope and always have confidence in Jesus and so that our desire to become more closely united to the Heart of Jesus may become stronger every day.

3. The Coming of the Holy Spirit upon Mary, the Apostles and the Others

On Pentecost all those assembled in the Upper Room were filled with the Holy Spirit. Mary was in the midst of that early

Church as Mother and as a disciple of Jesus, praying with the Church for the coming of the Holy Spirit. Mary will pray with us today, in power, as she prayed with that early Church , if we but ask her. Jesus wants us to use the prayers of Mary's Heart because they are so powerful and because they correspond so completely to His Will. He has given her to us especially as the Mother of the Church so that by the prayers of her motherly Heart she will care for us as her children and obtain for us the same evangelical zeal of that early Church.

Mary, give us your Heart so that we, too, like that early Church may be filled with the Holy Spirit and the courage to bring the Gospel message to all we meet.

4. The Assumption

Mary was assumed into heaven, body and soul. Jesus wanted her motherly Heart to be in heaven with His Heart because He determined that it was necessary for her Heart to participate in the salvation of all. The love of God comes to us from the Heart of Jesus as its source. This love requires a response and even though Mary's Heart is in heaven, she can give her Heart to us on earth in a spiritual way. To use Mary's Heart to respond to the love of Jesus is a perfect way because we use her Heart who always responded wholeheartedly. St. Ambrose said back in the 4th century, "Let the Heart of Mary be in every Christian".

Mary, we ask you to give us your Heart so that our response to the love of Jesus may always be wholehearted and pure.

5. The Coronation

Mary was crowned by Jesus as Queen of heaven and earth. Nothing can compare to the Eternal Word emptying Himself to take on a human nature. Yet, Mary's humility was so profound that, as St. Louis de Montfort tells us, the angels have never been able to find the limit of it, even though he knew that because she is only a creature, it is somehow limited. Jesus said, "He who exalts himself shall be humbled and he who humbles himself shall be exalted". Because of the greatness of the humility of Mary's Heart, Jesus exalted her as Queen above all of the angels and saints.

Mary, we ask you to give us your humble Heart so that we may acquire your humility while on earth and so that we may one day, too, be exalted by Jesus in heaven.

CHAPTER
X

THE IMMACULATE HEART (PRO-LIFE) MYSTERIES OF THE ROSARY

The Immaculate Heart (Pro-Life) Joyful Mysteries of the Rosary

1. The Annunciation

The angel Gabriel asked Mary if she wished to become the Mother of Him from whom all life comes. When she realized that this message was from God, Mary responded with the complete opening of her Heart and a total yes.

Mary, your response to God was to welcome Jesus, who is identified as Life, to your Immaculate Heart and to our earth. May the prayers of our hearts united with the prayers of your Immaculate Heart help mothers who are considering abortion to open their hearts and make a decision to welcome Jesus and the life and not the death of their unborn child!

2. The Visitation

When Mary found out from the angel, that her cousin, Elizabeth, was pregnant in her sixth month, she, without hesitation, went to help her in whatever way she could. When Mary arrived, Jesus, who was Life, itself, within her, touched the heart of Elizabeth and the life within her so that her baby leaped for joy.

Mary, we bring your presence and the prayers of your Heart to the mothers who are considering abortion so that Jesus, who you always bring with you, may touch the heart of each mother and cause the child within her to somehow influence that mother to save her baby's life. Help us to act without hesitation to help these mothers in whatever way we can!

3. The Birth of Jesus

In the midst of many hardships and the barest of material goods Mary and Joseph welcomed the one who created all, to creation, itself. The treasure that Jesus wanted was not the material goods of creation to live in but the treasure of open and welcoming hearts which Mary and Joseph provided for Him.

Mary, with what joy and love of your hearts did you and Joseph welcome the

Life of the world to this earth. We ask you to help these mothers, and fathers also, to understand, by the prayers of your heart, that even though this pregnancy may seem to be an insurmountable hardship for them, that God has given them a great gift, the gift of life. If they welcome this gift into their lives, God will find a way to work things out!

4.   The Presentation in the Temple

Mary and Joseph offered Jesus in Consecration to the Father in obedience to the Jewish law. Simeon prophesied that although the child would be the salvation for all the nations to see and a light for the pagans, he was destined to be rejected and that a sword of sorrow would pierce the Heart of Mary. Although this message was tinged with this prophecy of sorrow, the parents were filled with joy and peace at this Consecration because they knew that they were doing exactly what God wanted them to do.

Mary, your Heart, though wounded, was essentially joyful because your faith and hope told you that whatever happened in the future would only end in a good result for your Child and yourself. We ask you, with the prayers of your Heart, to help mothers who are considering an abortion to find the faith and hope that a good result will come about in their lives if they save their baby's life!

5. The Finding in the Temple

After a heart rending search, Mary and Joseph found Jesus in the temple. The loss Mary felt pre-figured the loss she was to feel at his death and burial. When mothers decide to allow their babies to be killed, they are, in reality, deciding to kill Jesus again as Jesus identifies Himself with each unborn child. The joy that Mary felt at Jesus' finding pre-figured the joy she would feel at his Resurrection.

Mary, we ask you, with the prayers of your Heart, to help these mothers about to have an abortion to feel somehow the enormity of the evil they are committing and give them the faith and courage to turn away from this evil, reject it, and find joy and peace in the saving of their baby's life!

The Immaculate Heart (Pro-Life) Mysteries of Light of the Rosary

1. The Baptism of Jesus

Jesus' consecrated Himself to the Father at His Baptism as He identified with sinners and was anointed by the Holy Spirit for His mission. The Scriptures do not tell us that Mary was present for the Baptism, but she always exemplified the meaning of Baptism in her life by opening her Heart completely to whatever God wanted her to do and then doing it wholeheartedly.

Mary, we ask you, with the prayers of your Heart, to help all pregnant mothers who are tempted to get an abortion, to open their hearts, so that they can identify the killing of their child as a serious sin and cause them to save their baby's life.

2. The Wedding Feast at Cana

Jesus, by virtue of His miracle in changing the water into a superabundance of wine, was to foreshadow the superabundance of the life of grace that would be available in the New Covenant. This grace would be available through the intercession of His Mother as He worked a miracle through her intercession at the wedding feast.

Mary, we ask you, with the prayers of your Heart, to intercede for the babies whose mothers are planning to kill them by abortion and obtain the miracle of grace needed to touch the hearts of their mothers and spare their lives.

3. The Proclamation of the Coming of the Kingdom of God

Jesus said at the beginning of the Gospel of Mark, "Repent and believe in the Gospel." The proclamation of the Gospel is accompanied by a call to conversion of life and sums up the entire Gospel message.

Mary, we ask you to help mothers who are considering an abortion, with the prayers of your Heart, to have a conversion of their own heart and make a decision for the life of their baby.

4. The Transfiguration

At the Transfiguration, the Divinity of Jesus is revealed. This is done so that Peter, James and John may be strengthened for the difficult times that would lie ahead. They hear the voice of the Father that they must listen to Jesus.

Mary, with the prayers of your Heart, obtain for those mothers who are considering an abortion, the ears to listen with their hearts to the words of Jesus, as he repeated the words of the Fifth Commandment, "You shall not kill" (Mt. 19: 18), and the strength to save their babies' lives.

5. The Last Supper

At the Mass the one Sacrifice of Jesus on the Cross is made present for us so that we can unite our hearts and lives with His one Sacrifice. The Eucharist must be the center of our spiritual warfare in the battles for human life. It must be the means for us as pro-life warriors to unite with each other in applying the victory over death which Jesus has already won.

Mary, by the prayers of your Heart, we ask you to help us always to find in Jesus in the Eucharist, the strength we need to defeat the powers of death. Help us always to make Jesus in the Eucharist the center of our pro-life efforts and prayers.

The Immaculate Heart
(Pro-Life)
Sorrowful Mysteries
of the Rosary

1. The Agony in the Garden

Jesus suffered the bloody sweat in the garden at the horrible thought and burden of our sins and the sins of the world. The murders connected with the sins of abortion and the rejection of Him who is Life, itself, caused His Heart special suffering. Mary knew in her Heart that something dreadful was happening to Jesus and she watched and waited in prayer. She sensed that she, too was an object of sin and that Jesus needed the full cooperation of her Heart in His work of salvation.

Mary, we ask you to help mothers who are considering an abortion, with the power of the prayers of your Heart, to realize the horror of abortion, to give them a hatred of that sin and a love for the life of their unborn child.

2. The Scourging at the Pillar

Mary knew that atonement for sins of the flesh and her purity and virginity were somehow intimately connected with this unbelievably painful lashing which left the flesh of her Son in bloody shreds. We know that it is very often, sins of impurity, especially fornication, that lead into the decision to get an abortion.

Mary give us your Heart so that we may love purity and chastity with the love of your Heart and so provide consolation to the Heart of Jesus for all the sins of the flesh being committed in the world today and especially those which end in the killing and torn body of the unborn child through abortion.

3.   The Crowning with Thorns

The crown of thorns was pushed cruelly into the head of Jesus causing Him grievous suffering. This was Satan's hour of supreme mockery as Jesus was mocked as a false King as the evil one had mocked God after the sin of Adam and Eve. These were acts of the highest pride and it is pride which is at the root of the sin of abortion. The mother is not listening to God who, by means of the natural law, has written on her heart, **"You shall not kill"**. She prefers to follow the suggestion of Satan as Eve had done in the Garden of Eden.

Mary, with the prayers of your Heart, help mothers to follow God's Commandment, forbidding the killing of their unborn child, written into the heart of every mother. Help them to achieve your humility so that they will open their hearts to believe that the life inside of them must be protected and not put to death.

4. Jesus Carries His Cross

Jesus embraced His Cross because it was the expression of the salvation of mankind and of His love for all human persons, including mothers who would make a decision to kill their child. Jesus knew that for His saving effort to be fully effective He had to reach Calvary. He knew that He could count on the love and courage of Mary's Heart to help Him persevere and reach His goal.

Mary, with the prayers of your Heart, help mothers who are considering an abortion, to obtain love for their unborn child and the courage to persevere in a decision to save their baby's life.

5. The Crucifixion and Death of Jesus

Jesus' Heart was filled with love for all men and in a special way for mothers and their unborn children. He knew that many mothers would reject His love and commit the terrible sin of abortion, risking their eternal salvation by the killing of their children. From the Cross He lovingly made His own Mother the spiritual Mother of the entire human race and allowed her to undergo the unspeakable suffering of a martyr's death so that as many souls as possible could be saved.

Mary, with the prayers of your Heart, help the mothers about to have an abortion realize that their eternal salvation is at risk. Help those mothers who have had an abortion to come to a sincere repentance and then to throw themselves upon the infinite mercy of God and if they are Catholic to believe that they must be forgiven in the Sacrament of Reconciliation.

The Immaculate Heart (Pro-Life) Glorious Mysteries of the Rosary

1. The Resurrection

The Resurrection presents for us a mystery of faith and confirms our faith in Jesus' Divinity and His Mission. His Mother, Mary, never stopped believing in Jesus and everything He said and did. Her faith was rewarded at the Resurrection and Jesus gave her the joy that always comes with persevering faith.

Mary, with the prayers of your Heart, we ask you to obtain for mothers who are seeking an abortion, the grace to believe that the life inside of them is a gift from God no matter how that baby came to be conceived. Help mothers to believe that God has given life to their babies and find joy in the belief that this life must be preserved and not destroyed.

2. The Ascension

The Ascension presents for us a mystery of hope. The supernatural virtue of hope is a desire to be with Jesus forever in eternity. On the natural level, hope is a desire for things to turn out better in a person's life even though things may appear to be hopeless. The Heart of Mary, although tempted to discouragement, never lost hope and always expressed the utmost confidence in every thing Jesus said and did.

Mary, with the prayers of your Heart, obtain hope for mothers seeking an abortion so that they may, with confidence, believe that bringing forth the birth of their child is the right thing to do for their lives.

3. The Coming of the Holy Spirit upon Mary, the Apostles and the Others

On Pentecost all those assembled in the upper room were filled with the Holy Spirit. Mary was in the midst of that early Church as a disciple of Jesus and as Mother of the Church, praying with the Church for the coming of the Holy Spirit.

By the prayers of her motherly Heart combined with the prayers of the others, those in the upper room were filled by the Holy Spirit, with the courage and evangelical zeal to proclaim the Gospel message.

Mary, by the prayers of your Heart, obtain for us the same courage and evangelical zeal of the early Church so that we may proclaim the message of the Gospel of Life which our Holy Father, Pope John Paul II, has told us, is the same as that of the Gospel of God's love for man and the Gospel of the dignity of the human person.[1]

4. The Assumption

Mary was taken up into heaven, body and soul. Jesus wanted her Immaculate Heart to be in heaven with His Sacred Heart because he determined that it was necessary for her Heart to participate in the salvation of all. The love of God comes to us from the Heart of Jesus as its source. This love requires a response and even though Mary's Heart is in heaven, she can give her Heart to us on earth in a spiritual way. To use Mary's Heart to respond to the love of Jesus is a perfect way because we use her Heart who always responded wholeheartedly. St. Ambrose said back in the 4th century, "Let the Heart of Mary be in every Christian".

Mary we ask you to give us your Heart so that our response to the love of Jesus and our pro-life efforts may always be wholehearted and pure.

5. The Coronation

Mary was crowned Queen of heaven and earth by Jesus. Nothing can compare to the Eternal Word emptying Himself to take on a human nature. Yet, Mary's humility was so profound that, as St. Louis de Montfort tells us, the angels have never been able to find the limit of it, even though he knew that because she is only a creature, it is somehow limited. Jesus said, "He who exalts himself shall be humbled and he who humbles himself shall be exalted". Because of the greatness of the humility of Mary's Heart, Jesus exalted her as Queen above all of the angels and saints.

Mary, we ask you to give us your humble Heart so that in our pro-life work we may acquire your humility and so give glory to God in all that we do.

NOTES

1.   Pope John Paul II, Papal Encyclical, **THE GOSPEL OF LIFE**, Random House, Inc., N.Y., N.Y., 1995, p.5

Printed in the United States
205533BV00003B/1-30/P